I0695819

Illuminating Oratory

Ignite Your Passion with Quotes

by

Henry Ukazu

&

Abdulakeem Sodeeq Sulyman

Dedication

This book is dedicated to every great individuals and leaders that have championed noble causes globally, either through their words or actions.

Our generation hugely owes them the credit of researching their works and place them where they deserve. Posterity must also acknowledge them and regard them in high esteem.

Acknowledgment

Compiling the quotes in this book would never be possible without the remarkable insights, resilience and sacrifices of individuals who believed that our world deserved to be better than it is and they pioneered the changes they wished to happen to our world.

We acknowledged every inventor, creator, innovator and intelligentsia for using their gifts, talents and passions to instil hopes in us and inspire us to be worthy examples to everyone around us.

Thank you!!!

Table of Content

<u>Adam Grant</u>

Years ago, psychologists discovered that there are two routes to achievement: conformity and originality. Conformity means following the crowd down conventional paths and maintaining the status quo. Originality is taking the road less traveled, championing a set of novel ideas that go against the grain but ultimately make things better." – Adam Grant

Consider the four responses to dissatisfaction: exit, voice, persistence and neglect. Only exit and voice improve your circumstances. Speaking up may be the best route if you have some control over the situation; if not, it may be time to explore options for expanding your influence or leaving." – Adam Grant

Leaders who don't have time to read are leaders who don't make time to learn." – Adam Grant

Originality itself starts with creativity: generating a concept that is both novel and useful. But it doesn't stop there. Originals are people who take initiative to make their visions a reality." – Adam Grant

The starting point is curiosity: pondering why the defaults exists in the first place. We're driven to question defaults when we experience vuja de, the opposite of déjà vu. Déjà vu occurs when we encounter something new, but it feels as if we have seen it before. Vuja de is the reverse — we face something familiar, but we see it with a fresh perspective that enables us to gain new insights into old problems." – Adam Grant

When we become curious about the dissatisfying defaults in our world, we begin to recognize that most of them have social origins: Rules and systems were created by people. And that awareness gives us the courage to contemplate how we can change them." – Adam Grant

In every domain, from business and politics to science and art, the people who move the world forward with original ideas are rarely paragons of conviction and commitment." – Adam Grant

To become original, you have to try something new, which means accepting some measure of risk. But the most successful originals are not the daredevils who leap before they look. They are the ones who reluctantly tiptoe to the edge of a cliff, calculate the rate of descent, tripple—check their parachutes, and set up a safety net at the bottom just in case!" – Adam Grant

The greatest presidents were those who challenged the status quo and brought about sweeping changes that improved the lot of the country." – Adam Grant

Originality is not a fixed trait. It is a free choice...jobs are not static sculptures, but flexible building blocks." – Adam Grant

What sets original people apart is that they take action anyway. They know in their hearts that failing would yield less regret than failing to try." – Adam Grant

When we bemoan the lack of originality in the world, we blame it on the absence of creativity. If only people could generate more novel ideas, we'd all be better off. But in reality, the biggest barrier to originality is not idea generation — it is idea selection." – Adam Grant

To some degree, entrepreneurs and inventors have to be overconfident about the odds of their ideas succeeding, or they wouldn't have the motivational fuel to pursue them." – Adam Grant

Many people fail to achieve originality because they generate a few ideas and then obsess about refining them to perfection." – Adam Grant

Conviction in our ideas is dangerous not only because it leaves us vulnerable to false positives, but also because it stops us from generating the requisite variety to reach our creative potential." – Adam Grant

The annals of corporate innovation are filled with tales of managers ordering employees to stop working on projects that turned out to be big hits..." – Adam Grant

It is when people have moderate expertise in a particular domain that they are most open to radically creative ideas." – Adam Grant

...being a creator in one particular area doesn't make you a great forecaster in others. To accurately predict the success of a novel idea, it is best to be a creator in the domain you are judging." – Adam Grant

If you stop and take time to think, it is easy to lose the forest in the trees." – Adam Grant

Power involves exercising control or authority over others; status is being respected and admired." – Adam Grant

Middle – status conformity leads us to choose the safety of the tried – and – true over the danger of the original." – Adam Grant

Procrastination may be the enemy of productivity, but it can be a resource for creativity." – Adam Grant

Long before the modern obsession with efficiency precipitated by the Industrial Revolution and the Protestant work ethic, civilization recognized the benefits of procrastination. In ancient Egypt, there were two different verbs for procrastination: one denoted laziness; the other meant waiting for the right time." – Adam Grant

You cannot produce a work of genius according to a schedule or outline." – Adam Grant

Being original doesn't require being first. It just means being different and better." – Adam Grant

The more experiments you run, the less constrained you become by your ideas from the past." – Adam Grant

...our best allies aren't the people who have supported us all along. They are the ones who started out against us and then came around to our side." – Adam Grant

Birth order doesn't determine who you are; it only affects the probability that you will develop in a particular way..." – Adam Grant

It is easier to start a relationship with the door open than to try open a door that's already been slammed shut." – Adam Grant

A principle is just some type of event happening over and over again, and how to deal with that event." – Adam Grant

The greatest shapers don't stop at introducing originality into the world. They create cultures that unleash originality in others." – Adam Grant

Choosing to challenge the status quo is an uphill battle, and there are bound to be failures, barriers, and setbacks along the way." – Adam Grant

Originality brings more bumps in the road, yet it leaves us with more happiness and a greater sense of meaning." – Adam Grant

The most inspiring way to convey a vision is to outsource it to the people who are actually affected by it." – Adam Grant

If you want people to modify their behaviour, it is better to highlight the benefits of changing or the costs of not changing." – Adam Grant

When we are determined to reach an objective, it's the gap between where we are and where we aspire to be that lights a fire under us." – Adam Grant

Becoming original is not the easiest path in the pursuit of happiness, but it leaves us perfectly poised for the happiness of pursuit." – Adam Grant

Charisma attracts attention. Courage earns admiration. But commitment to a group inspires loyalty." – Adam Grant

Instead of seeking out friendly people who share your values, try approaching disagreeable people who share your methods." – Adam Grant

In the face of injustice, thinking about the perpetrator fuels the anger and aggression. Shifting your attention to the victim makes you more empathetic, increasing the chances that you'll channel your anger in a constructive direction. Instead of trying to punish the people who caused harm, you'll be more likely to help the people who were harmed." – Adam Grant

<u>Albert Einstein</u>

Great spirits have always encountered opposition from mediocre minds." – Albert Einstein

Education is not the learning of facts, but the training of the mind to think." – Albert Einstein

Imagination is the preview of what is to happen." – Albert Einstein

Only one who devotes himself to a cause with his whole strength and soul can be a true master. For this reason, mastery demands all of a person." – Albert Einstein

Great spirits have always encountered violent opposition from mediocre minds. The mediocre mind is incapable of understanding the man who refuses to bow blindly to conventional prejudices and chooses instead to express his opinions courageously and honestly." – Albert Einstein

If you can't explain something simply, you don't understand it well enough." – Albert Einstein

If you want to live a happy life, tie it to a goal, not to people or things." – Albert Einstein

The primary requirement for solving a problem is to change the way we think about it." – Albert Einstein

I am truly a 'lone—traveller' and never belonged to my country, my home, my friends, or even my immediate family with my whole heart. In face of all these ties, I have never lost a sense of distance and a need for solitude, feeling that increase with the year." – Albert Einstein

He who can no longer pause to wonder and stand rapt in awe, is as good as dead; his eyes are close." — Albert Einstein

Never give up on what you really want to do. The person with big dreams is more powerful than one with all the facts." – Albert Einstein

If I were given one hour to save the planet, I would spend 59 minutes defining the problem and one minute resolving it." – Albert Einstein

It's not that I'm so smart, it's just that I stay with problems longer." — Albert Einstein

The intuitive mind is a sacred gift, and the rational mind is a faithful servant." – Albert Einstein

Good times create weak people; weak people create bad times. Bad times create strong people; strong people create good times." – Anthony Robbins

Clearly—defined goals mean that you become focused in a certain direction and from there on your thoughts and actions will be directed, consciously and unconsciously, towards that outcome." – Anthony Robbins

Goals might be defined as dreams with a deadline. It's important to set a time frame on the achievement of goals, give yourself a deadline. Scrutinise your actions constantly to analyse their relevance to your goals. Put pen to paper and dare to dream." – Anthony Robbins

Successful people spend 10% of their time focused on the problems and 90% of the rest, focused on the solution." – Anthony Robbins

Perfection is not heroism, but humanity is. Within each of us burns the spark of heroism and we can fan into flame if we choose." – Anthony Robbins

To live a rich life, you need more than just success. You need to live. And living requires fulfillment, not just achievement. Fulfillment comes from finding what makes you happy, what brings you joy." – Anthony Robbins

It's in your moments of decision that your destiny is shaped."
– Anthony Robbins

The secret to wealth is simple, find a way to do more for others than anyone else does. Become more valuable. Do more. Be more. Serve more. And you will have the opportunity to earn more." – Anthony Robins

I find out what works, and then I clarify it, simplify it, and systematize it—in a way to help people move forward!" – Anthony Robbins

All personal breakthroughs begin with a change in beliefs." – Anthony Robbins

It is not what we do once in a while that shapes our lives. It is what we do on a consistent basis." – Anthony Robbins

Aristotle

Happiness is the actualisation of our potential in activities of moral and intellectual virtue. Happiness is human flourishing — not happy feelings." – Aristotle

The point of politics is to moderate bad government so that it doesn't become worse and, if possible, to try to gradually make it better." – Aristotle

It is well to be up before daybreak, for such habits contribute to health, wealth and wisdom." — Aristotle

All human actions have one or more of these seven causes: chance, nature, compulsions, habit, reason, passion, desire." – Aristotle

Anybody can become angry — that is easy; but to be angry with the right person, and to the right degree, and at the right time, and for the right purpose, and in the right way — that is not within everybody's power and is not easy." – Aristotle

Excellence is an art won by training and habituation. We do not act rightly because we have virtue or excellence, but rather we have those because we have acted rightly. We are what we repeatedly do. Excellence, then, is not an act but a habit." – Aristotle

It is the mark of an educated mind to be able to entertain a thought without accepting it." – Aristotle

Once the potentialities for morality are developed and internalised in the individual, they become an integral part of his social identity, automatically expressed and acted upon, without the individual going through the routine processes of ratiocination or piecemeal calculation." – Aristotle

Goodness is never in the action but only in the actor." – Aristotle

For what is the best choice, for each individual, is the highest it is possible for him to achieve." – Aristotle

No one is born immoral, it is the choices that we make after birth that make us either moral or immoral." – Aristotle

Man is a noblest animal; separated from law and justice, he is the worst." – Aristotle

Those who educate children well are more to be honored than parents, for these only gave life, those the art of living well." – Aristotle

Arnold Schwarzenegger

It is only losers that fails and stay down. When winners fail, they get up." – Arnold Schwarzenegger

Don't be afraid to fail; if you are afraid to fail, you are getting yourself frozen and stifled." – Arnold Schwarzenegger

What you do is create a vision of who you want to be, and then live into that picture as if it were already true." – Arnold Schwarzenegger

Strength does not come from winning; your struggles develop your strengths. When you go through hardships and decide not to surrender, that is strength." – Arnold Schwarzenegger

It is only losers that fails and stay down. When winners fail, they get up." – Arnold Schwarzenegger

Don't be afraid of failing because if you do, you get yourself frozen." – Arnold Schwarzenegger

Barack Obama

Something like this is just part of growing up. And sometimes growing up hurts." – Barack Obama

You are fortunate if you have parents who inspire you to seek for knowledge, inspiring curiosity, even if they are not super—highly educated..." – Barack Obama

Building the future that you see, the vision that you have – not just for yourself, but your country – would not going to be easy." – Barack Obama

The path we follow may be hard, but it leads to a better place." – Barack Obama

During political campaigns, truths are always buried under the avalanche of money and advertising." – Barack Obama

Building strong, qualitative education is not what the government alone can do. To do that, principals must lead, teachers must inspire, parents should instill the thirst for learning in children. We all have roles to play..." – Barack Obama

Change will not come if we wait for some other person or some other time. We are the ones we've been waiting for. We are the change that we seek." – Barrack Obama

...we are not entitled to success. We are to earn it." – Barack Obama

We don't think that government can solve all of our problems, but we always think government is the cause of all our problems." – Barack Obama

The elections four years ago were not about me, but about you. My fellow citizens, you are the change." – Barack Obama

As citizens, we understand that America is not about what can be done for us, it is about what can be done by us together." – Barack Obama

America's vision has never been about what can be done for us; but what can be done by us, together for us..." – Barack Obama

The role of citizens in every democracy doesn't end with your vote." – Barack Obama

No matter how successful one has been, there is always much to do, more to learn, more to know and more to achieve." – Barack Obama

In your own life, you have to continuously adapt to a continuously changing economy." – Barack Obama

You have to be determined to meet the time on your own terms." – Barack Obama

Find somebody you should be successful for; raise their hopes and rise to their needs." – Barack Obama

Professors may have more than ten years of academic excellence and distinctions. Bu that doesn't determine that they spent long hours of the night to fill their drive and passion to be great educators." – Barack Obama

Being a parent is more than mere bringing the child to the world, but an act of love and sacrifice to raise and educate that child." – Barack Obama

You can't create a story that moves large number of people, unless you listen to the story of the people next to you." – Barack Obama

To be black was to be the beneficiary of a great inheritance, a special destiny, glorious burdens that only we were strong enough to bear." – Barack Obama

For I'm convinced that the pandemic we're currently living through is both a manifestation of and a mere interruption in the relentless march toward an interconnected world, one in which peoples and cultures can't help but collide." – Barack Obama

Politics doesn't have to be what people think it is. It can be something more." – Barack Obama

Sometimes you can't worry about hurt. Sometimes you worry only about getting where you have to go." – Barack Obama

One of the most important things about the nature of work is that it is never exhausted; it is cumulative, it expands your knowledge base and deepens your horizon of learning, every day you gives it your best." – Barack Obama

The most effective debate answers, it seemed, were designed not to illuminate but to evoke an emotion, or identify the enemy, or signal to a constituency that you, more than anyone else on that stage, were and would always be on their side." – Barack Obama

In presidential politics, the best strategy means little if you don't have the resources to execute it, and this was the second thing we had going for us: money." – Barack Obama

We know the battle ahead will be long, but always remember that no matter what obstacles stand in our way, nothing can stand in the way of the power of millions of voices calling for change." – Barack Obama

When we've been told we're not ready," I said, "or that we shouldn't try, or that we can't, generations of Americans have responded with a simple creed that sums up the spirit of a people: Yes we can." – Barack Obama

There is not a liberal America and a conservative America. There is not a Black America and a white America and a Latino America and an Asian America. There's the United States of America." – Barack Obama

If you look at the world and look at the problems it's usually old people, usually old men, not getting out of the way." – Barack Obama

I don't oppose all wars, what I am opposed to is a dumb war." – Barack Obama

Change requires more than just speaking out; it requires listening as well." – Barack Obama

...there are people in the world who think only about themselves. They don't care what happens to other people so long as they get what they want. They put other people down to make themselves feel important. Then there are people who do the opposite, who are able to imagine how others must feel, and make sure that they don't do things that hurt people." – Barack Obama

The truth is, I've never been a big believer in destiny. I worry that it encourages resignation in the down—and—out and complacency among the powerful." – Barack Obama

<u>Bill Gates</u>

Success is a lousy teacher. It makes smart people think they can't lose." – Bill Gates

If you are born poor, it is not your mistake, but if you die poor it is your mistake." – Bill Gates

I failed in some subjects in exam, but my friend passed in all. Now, he is an engineer in Microsoft and I am the owner of Microsoft." – Bill Gates

Every book teaches me something new or helps me see things differently. Reading fuels a sense of curiosity about the world, which I think helped drive me forward in my career." – Bill Gates

Your most unhappy customers are your greatest source of learning." – Bill Gates

Most people overestimate what they can do in one year and underestimate what they can do in ten years." — Bill Gates

Everyone needs a coach. We all need people that give us feedback. That's how we improve." – Bill Gates

<u>**Brian Tracy**</u>

Time management is essential for maximum health and personal effectiveness. The degree to which you feel in control of your time and your life is a major determinant of your level of inner peace, harmony, and mental well—being." – Brian Tracy

You can only grow if you are willing to feel awkward and uncomfortable when you try something new." – Brian Tracy

My life is precious and important, and I value every single minute and hour of it. I am going to use those hours properly so that I accomplish the most I can, in the time that I have." – Brian Tracy

The Law of Control says that you feel good about yourself to the degree to which you feel you are in control of your own life. This law also says that you feel negative about yourself to the degree to which you feel that you are not in control of your own life or work." – Brian Tracy

Move out of your comfort zone. You can only grow if you are willing to feel awkward and uncomfortable when you try something new." – Brian Tracy

There is a big difference between action that is self—determined and goal—directed and reaction, which is an immediate response to external pressure. It's the difference between feeling positive and in control of your life and feeling negative, stressed, and pressured." – Brian Tracy

...your self—concept causes you to continually strive for consistency between the person you see yourself as, on the inside, and the way you perform on the outside." – Brian Tracy

Every change in your life comes about when you make a clear, unequivocal decision to do something differently." – Brian Tracy

Good time management requires that you bring your control over a sequence of events into harmony with what is most important to you. If it is not important to you, then you will never feel motivated and determined to get control of your time." – Brian Tracy

One of the major reasons for personal stress and unhappiness is the feeling that what you are doing has no meaning and purpose as it applies to you and your innermost values and convictions." – Brian Tracy

Almost all stress, tension, anxiety, and frustration, both in life and in work, comes from doing one thing while you believe and value something completely different." – Brian Tracy

Before you step on the accelerator of your own life, you must develop absolute clarity about what you are really trying to accomplish." – Brian Tracy

If all you are working for is to earn enough money to pay your bills, it's going to be hard for you to build up and maintain a high level of commitment and enthusiasm. To be truly happy and fulfilled, you must be working toward accomplishing something that is bigger than yourself, and that makes a difference in the life or work of others." – Brian Tracy

One common thread that I discovered in the biographies and autobiographies I have read was that true greatness only emerges with introspection, retrospection, solitude, and contemplation." – Brian Tracy

You will only achieve the greatness you are capable of when you begin to take time regularly to think about who you are, what you want, and the very best way to achieve it." – Brian Tracy

When you are clear about where you want to be sometime in the future, it is much easier for you to make better decisions in the present. The rule is that long—term vision improves short—term decision making. You have heard the saying, 'If you don't know where you're going, any road will get you there.'" – Brian Tracy

Once you are clear about your goal, you then make a list of everything that you can think of that you will have to do to achieve that goal." – Brian Tracy

Perhaps the most important word related to success of any kind is clarity. Successful people are very clear about who they are and what they want, in every area of their lives." – Brian Tracy

Remember that what gets measured gets done. A goal without a deadline is not really a goal. It is merely a discussion." – Brian Tracy

Those people who develop the ability to continuously acquire new and better forms of knowledge that they can apply to their work and to their lives will be the movers and shakers in our society for the indefinite future." – Brian Tracy

Remember, the most wonderful talent you have is your ability to think, especially to think things through in advance. The more time you take to think and plan, on paper, the better results you will get, and the faster you will get those results." – Brian Tracy

Each person is a creature of habit. Effective people establish good habits and make them their masters. Ineffective people accidentally establish bad habits, and then those bad habits govern their lives." – Brian Tracy

In your work, there are things that only you can do. If you don't do them, no one else will do them for you. If you do them well, it will make an extraordinary difference to your job and to your company. These are the specific activities that contribute the greatest value to your work." – Brian Tracy

...if you cannot concentrate on one thing at a time, then you cannot be successful. You need to do first things first, one thing at a time, and second things not at all. If you do not discipline yourself to concentrate single—mindedly, you will invariably find yourself working on low—priority tasks." – Brian Tracy

...each time you put down a task and turn to something else, you lose momentum and rhythm, and you lose track of where you were in doing that job. When you come back to the task, you have no choice but to review your previous work, catch up to the point where you were when you broke off, and then begin again." – Brian Tracy

The high producer procrastinates on tasks and activities of low or no value. The low producer procrastinates on tasks that have considerable value to the company and to the individual's own career. For you to produce at your maximum, you must resolve to engage in "creative procrastination" from this day forward." – Brian Tracy

It is not possible for you to keep current with your field and be on top of your industry unless you are feeding your mind, continually but selectively, with the information that is being generated today by some of the smartest people who ever lived." – Brian Tracy

The main purpose of learning and practicing time management skills is to enhance and improve the overall quality of your life." – Brian Tracy

The people you care about and who care about you are the most critical factors in your life. Never allow yourself to get so caught up in your work that you ignore the primacy of those key relationships with your spouse, children, and close friends." – Brian Tracy

Your choice of people you associate with will have more impact on what you become than any other single factor." – Brian Tracy

Your choice of people you associate with will have more impact on what you become than any other single factor." — Brian Tracy

...of all things that people do, thinking has the greatest possible consequences. The better you think, the better decisions you make. The better decisions you make, the better actions you will take. The better actions you take, the better results you will get, and the better will be the quality of your life and work. Everything begins with thinking." – Brian Tracy

The very best way to develop yourself is in the direction of your natural talents and interest." – Brian Tracy

Teamwork is so important that it is virtually impossible for you to reach the heights of your capabilities or make the money that you want without becoming very good at it." – Brain Tracy

<u>Carol S. Dweck</u>

Almost everyone, at one time or another, had been in love and had been hurt. What differed — and differed dramatically — was how they dealt with it." - Carol S. Dweck

Well, the course to true love is not so smooth, either. That path is often strewn with disappointments and heartbreaks. Some people let these experiences scar them and prevent them from forming satisfying relationship in the future." - Carol S. Dweck

...a good, lasting relationship comes from effort and from working through inevitable differences." - Carol S. Dweck

A no—effort relationship is a doomed relationship, not a great relationship. It takes work to communicate accurately and it takes work to expose and resolve conflicting hopes and beliefs." - Carol S. Dweck

David Schwartz

Belief, strong belief, triggers the mind to figure ways and means and how—to. And believing you can succeed makes others place confidence in you." - David Schwartz

It is well to respect the leader. Learn from him. Observe him. Study him. But don't worship him. Believe you can surpass. Believe you can go beyond. Those who harbor the second—best attitude are invariably second—best doers." - David Schwartz

Your mind is a "thought factory." It's a busy factory, producing countless thoughts in one day." - David Schwartz

Thinking success conditions your mind to create plans that produce success. Thinking failure does the exact opposite. Failure thinking conditions the mind to think other thoughts that produce failure." - David Schwartz

You already have a fully equipped laboratory in which you can work and study. Your laboratory is all around you. Your laboratory consists of human beings. This laboratory supplies you with every possible example of human action. And there is no limit to what you can learn once you see yourself as a scientist in your own lab." - David Schwartz

Each contact you make with another person gives you a chance to see success development principles at work. Your objective is to make successful action habitual." - David Schwartz

Study the lives of successful people and you'll discover this: all the excuses made by the mediocre fellow could be but aren't made by the successful persons." – David Schwartz

Thoughts, positive or negative, grow stronger when fertilized with constant repetition." – David Schwartz

The thinking that guides your intelligence is much more important than the quantity of your brainpower." – David Schwartz

...how old we are is not important. It's one's attitude toward age that makes it a blessing or a barricade." – David Schwartz

Age has no real relation to ability, unless you convince yourself that years alone will give you the stuff you need to make your mark." – David Schwartz

Look at things not as they are, but as they can be. Visualization adds value to everything. A big thinker always visualizes what can be done in the future." – David Schwartz

When you believe something is impossible, your mind goes to work for you to prove why. But when you believe, really believe, something can be done, your mind goes to work for you and helps you find the ways to do it." — David Schwartz

Many of us whip and defeat our desires simply because we concentrate on why we can't when the only thing worthy of our mental concentration is why we can." – David Schwartz

Nothing grows in ice. If we let tradition freeze our minds, new ideas can't sprout." – David Schwartz

A leader is a decision—making human machine. Now, to manufacture anything, you've got to have raw material. In reaching creative decisions, the raw materials are the ideas and suggestions of others. Don't, of course, expect other people to give you ready—made solutions. That's not the primary reason for asking and listening. Ideas of others help to spark your own ideas so your mind is more creative." - David Schwartz

There is no surer way to get people to like you than to encourage them to talk to you." - David Schwartz

Listening is more than just keeping your own mouth shut. Listening means letting what's said penetrate your mind." - David Schwartz

Remember, a mind that feeds only on itself soon is undernourished, becoming weak and incapable of creative progressive thought. Stimulation from others is excellent mind food." - David Schwartz

Memory is a weak slave when it comes to preserving and nurturing brand—new ideas." - David Schwartz

The kind of mind food we consume determines our habits, attitudes, personality. Each of us inherited a certain capacity to develop. But how much of that capacity we have developed and the way we have developed that capacity depends on the kind of mind food we feed it." - David Schwartz

Prolonged association with negative people makes us think negatively; close contact with petty individuals develops petty habits in us. On the bright side, companionship with people with big ideas raises the level of our thinking; close contact with ambitious people gives us ambition." – David Schwartz

People who tell you it cannot be done almost always are unsuccessful people, are strictly average or mediocre at best in terms of accomplishment. The opinions of these people can be poison." – David Schwartz

It is not possible to win high—level success without meeting opposition, hardship, and setback. But it is possible to use setbacks to propel you forward." – David Schwartz

It is true that in this complex world others may trip us. But it is also true that more often than not we trip ourselves. We lose because of personal inadequacy, some personal mistake." – David Schwartz

Balls don't bounce in certain ways for uncertain reasons. The bounce of a ball is determined by three things: the ball, the way it is thrown, and the surface it strikes. Definite physical laws explain the bounce of a ball, not luck." – David Schwartz

Persisting in one way is not a guarantee of victory. But persistence blended with experimentation does guarantee success." – David Schwartz

A problem, a difficulty, becomes unsolvable only when you think it is unsolvable. Attract solutions by believing solutions are possible." – David Schwartz

Real education, the kind worth investing in, is that which develops and cultivates your mind. How well educated a person is, is measured by how well his mind is developed—in brief, by how well he thinks." – David Schwartz

Deborah Tom and William Barrons

You may not like the military but that shouldn't stop you from learning from their mistakes and what they have learned to do right." – Deborah Tom and William Barrons

...the soul of an organisation is what makes it loose or win battles. Building soul is about getting the best from people at all levels of your organisation because the firm and its purpose matter to them." – Deborah Tom and William Barrons

Good training is not good if it remains no more than notes in a desk drawer." – Deborah Tom and William Barrons

Humans have imperfect perceptions, judgments and memory, and these can all affect the way facts are recorded for future reference." – Deborah Tom and William Barrons

Dilemmas are bound to occur in the minds of those who think. If you are not discussing dilemmas, it could be because people are not thinking deeply enough, merely complying, and with compliance comes lack of dynamic momentum." – Deborah Tom and William Barrons

You can't expect to win by being exclusively defensive. Sometimes encouraging an opponent to batter himself to a standstill against a strong defence may be the best route to victory..." – Deborah Tom and William Barrons

Soul is as fundamental as intellect, technology and physical strength in achieving success." – Deborah Tom and William Barrons

If you show your irritability and frustration at work, you are blackening the waters around you." – Deborah Tom and William Barrons

A leader who neglects or merely pays lip service to improving their emotional intelligence is unlikely to survive for long in a senior position in today's world." – Deborah Tom and William Barrons

Charisma is the gift of being able to inspire and influence. To be charismatic, you don't have to be larger–than–life, loud, colourful, extroverted personality; you don't have to be outrageous or set out deliberately to inspire others. Humble, quiet, clever, unassuming, ingenious people have plenty followers too; theirs is a quiet charisma." – Deborah Tom and William Barrons

The best organisations in any field rely heavily on the self–discipline of their staff, not only to do the simple things well, like turn up on time, but also to apply their time and talents to the full in order to add to their collective success." – Deborah Tom and William Barrons

Where you find individuals whose soul is disconnected from their actions or where the collective soul is absent, the seeds of that organisation's self–destruction will have been sown." – Deborah Tom and William Barrons

One way to really know someone is to 'see them in the middle of their lives' and understand where they have come from and where they want to go, as well as the complexities in their lives at present." – Deborah Tom and William Barrons

Self—efficacy refers to the judgment people make about their capability, whereas self—esteem is about the judgments people make about their sense of worth." – Deborah Tom and William Barrons

People who live their values feel better about themselves and make faster, better decisions." – Deborah Tom and William Barrons

If you focus too much on rational decision making, you will not develop your ability to trust your intuition." – Deborah Tom and William Barrons

The shape and culture of the organisation must match its purpose. Any endeavour that brings two or more people together requires some form of organisation." – Deborah Tom and William Barrons

It can be hard to turn theory into action in any environment, but having a well—formed and tested theory is at least a start." – Deborah Tom and William Barrons

The real 'creatives' are those who seize responsibility for an idea and make it happen." – Deborah Tom and William Barrons

Denzel Washington

Ease is the major threat to success, not hardship. Without commitment, you won't start. Without consistency, you won't finish." – Denzel Washington

You must not only be aspired to make a living, you must be inspired to make a difference." – Denzel Washington

Every failed experiment is one step closer to success..." – Denzel Washington

A mother is a son's first true love. While a son — most especially the first — is a mother's last true love." – Denzel Washington

Men give the awards; God gives the rewards." – Denzel Washington

Don't be afraid to be dream big. But remember, dreams are just dreams without goals." – Denzel Washington

Hard work works. Working really hard is what successful people do." – Denzel Washington

Remember, just because you are doing a lot more doesn't mean you will get a lot done. Don't confuse movement with progress." – Denzel Washington

Life is not always about how much you have; it is about what you do with what you had." – Denzel Washington

The most selfish thing you could do in this world is to help others. Why is helping others selfish? Because of the gratification you get from it, the good feeling you enjoy from helping someone else." – Denzel Washington

Don't just inspire to make a living; aspire to make a difference." – Denzel Washington

I don't understand the concept of 'have something to fall back on.' If I am going to fall, I don't want to fall on anything, I want to fall forward." – Denzel Washington

Every fail experiment is one step closer to success. You have to take risks because I have found that nothing is worthwhile in life unless you take risks." – Denzel Washington

If you don't fail, you aren't even trying. To get something you never had, you have to do something you never did." – Denzel Washington

<u>Donald J. Trump</u>

Don't limit yourself to staid thinking because you want to excel in business." – Donald J. Trump

Sometimes new ideas can come from something as mundane and functional as your windshield wipers. The key is to pay attention and keep your brain and senses open to new stimuli." – Donald J. Trump

One reason people like me is because I'm blunt. One reason people don't like me is because I'm blunt. But one reason I'm successful is that I can cut through nonsense quickly and get to the core of things." – Donald J. Trump

Be a great assembler — no matter what your interests may be — and you'll be on your way to inventiveness." – Donald J. Trump

A big mind requires a variety of thoughts and impulses to keep it well occupied, so make sure you keep your mind engaged in the best ways possible. It could very well be your calling card for success." – Donald J. Trump

Never negate the power of the team, and you'll be a team player of note as well as power." – Donald J. Trump

It's important to remain open to new ideas and new information. Being a know — it — all is like shutting the door to great discoveries and opportunities. Keep your door open every day to something new and energizing." – Donald J. Trump

...start every day with a clean slate. Give yourself a new beginning by opening up your mind." – Donald J. Trump

Never think of learning as being a burden or studying as being boring. It may require some discipline, but it can be an adventure. It can also prepare you for a new beginning." – Donald J. Trump

If you see every day as a challenge, you'd be surprised how efficient you can become and how much can be accomplished." – Donald J. Trump

Just because you don't see someone working doesn't mean they haven't been working in their spare or private time. I prepare myself thoroughly, and then when it is time to move ahead, I am ready to sprint." – Donald J. Trump

Thought without action won't amount to much in the long run. Those great ideas you have will remain great ideas unless you actively do something with them." – Donald J. Trump

You have to unplug before you can plug yourself back in." – Donald J. Trump

Life is a performance art, no matter what field you are in." – Donald J. Trump

Strive for wholeness and keep your sense of wonder intact, and you will find yourself ready for a grand slam." – Donald J. Trump

When the achiever achieves, it's not a plateau, it's a beginning. Achievers move forward at all times they have anticipation for their next deal and have another goal immediately lined up." – Donald J. Trump

Visionaries move the world along into new dimensions." – Donald J. Trump

Sometimes we do things to build up experience and stamina to prepare us, but it's to prepare us for something bigger. Always know you could be on the precipice of something great—that's being connected to your higher self. It's also a good way to keep those negative thoughts far away." – Donald J. Trump

Being industrious can be a magnet for new ideas, while idleness and inertia can be magnets for negativity." – Donald J. Trump

Life can be an adventure of the best sort if you will give your higher self a chance. We all have something unique to offer. Our work is to find out what that is and to work at it with a passion." – Donald J. Trump

...every day is another opportunity to learn something new." – Donald J. Trump

We are individually responsible for our education, and that applies whether you're in school or not." – Donald J Trump

...interesting aspect of history is that it will lead us to seeing that we are all a part of it. History isn't just in the past—it's happening now. How can you know what you're a part of if you don't know what it is to begin with?" – Donald J. Trump

The world didn't start with your birth, and it won't end with your death either." – Donald J. Trump

We win in our daily lives by being careful with every day, by having a champion's view of each moment." – Donald J. Trump

Don't fail because you never allowed yourself to get started! Don't avoid success because you think the responsibility might be too much—just focus and get going!" – Donald J. Trump

Art is not life, but it's about life. It can point to truths that we might not notice in our busy daily lives." – Donald J. Trump

Many topics come up in the course of a business discussion or interview, and while we can't know everything, we should know as much as we can." – Donald J. Trump

Creative thinking is a must these days. Make it work for you." – Donald J. Trump

If you label something as a fear, then it creates fear when sometimes it's not a fear but a concern." – Donald J. Trump

Fear creates a block that will only hinder your creative thinking. Objectivity will remove that block and allow for creative ideas to flow." – Donald J. Trump

Faith is one reason you've got to believe in yourself and see yourself as victorious." – Donald J. Trump

Sometimes people think things just happen overnight, but that's not always the case, even if you are well known and well established. Success is often a matter of patience, and patience can be developed if you don't have it naturally." – Donald J. Trump

To have a tight team, a winning team, you can't have someone who lags behind, because everyone will suffer because of it." – Donald J. Trump

Every day ask yourself what problems might arise, review every project yourself, and make sure you are on top of your own agenda." – Donald J. Trump

How we handle difficult situations in life says a lot about who we are. How we view them is also an important element in how we will deal with adversity." – Donald J. Trump

Problems, setbacks, mistakes, and losses are all a part of life. It's something we have to accept. We shouldn't be shocked if and when they happen." – Donald J. Trump

If you can't say great things about yourself, who do you think will?" – Donald J. Trump

...the more independent people become, the stronger a nation becomes as a whole." – Donald J. Trump

I've waited twenty years to see some things happen, but it was worth the wait and I had to change course a few times until the pieces finally fell into place. Destiny has a part to play in your life and in your business — so give it a chance to work." — Donald J. Trump

Sometimes one thing leads to another — that's a form of discovery. Discovery breeds discovery, as in success breeds success. Questions are thoughts with a quest." — Donald J. Trump

People who have endured great hardship often say they survived because they kept some sort of hope going, a vision of the future, despite horrible immediate circumstances. They may not have had a big picture in mind at the time, but they had a semblance of one." — Donald J. Trump

Sometimes a dead end can be a new beginning." — Donald J. Trump

If people waited for everything to be perfect before attempting anything, the world would be in a sorry state." — Donald J. Trump

If you see every day as an important day for your future and a special day just because you have it, you will be amazed at how productive and energetic you will be." — Donald J. Trump

No matter how good you are, when arrogance raises its ugly head, Mother Nature will put you back into your box." — Donald J. Trump

If your goal is just to make money, you are shortchanging yourself. You might also run out of energy while you're trying to make that money. Passion is an incredible source of fuel that can get you through the tough spells that are bound to come up." — Donald J. Trump

Efficiency is the productive use of time. Learn to monitor yourself and the amount of time you use to focus on any specific thing. Having a time limit can be a terrific way to make your brain work at its most effective pace." — Donald J. Trump

George Bernard Shaw

The reasonable man adapts himself to the world; the unreasonable one persists in trying to adapt the world to himself. Therefore all progress depends on the unreasonable man." — George Bernard Shaw

Successful people look around themselves and search for what they want. If they can't find it, they create one." — George Bernard Shaw

...when it comes to fulfilling your gifts, talents, admirable ambitions and instinct to change the world in whatever way must resonates with you, never, ever be reasonable with yourself." — George Bernard Shaw

There are three types of people in life: Those that make things happen, those that watch things happen and those who don't know what happen." — George Bernard Shaw

Some men see things as they are and say "why?" I dream of things that never were and say "why not?" — George Bernard Shaw

Some men see things as they are and say "why"; I dream of things that never were and say "why not." — George Bernard Shaw

He who can, does; he who cannot, teaches." — George Bernard Shaw

This is the true joy of life: the being used up for a purpose recognized by yourself as a mighty one; being a force of nature instead of a feverish, selfish little clot of ailments and grievances, complaining that the world will not devote itself to making you happy." — George Bernard Shaw

A life spent in making mistakes is not only more honorable but more useful than a life spent doing nothing." — George Bernard Shaw

Helen Keller

Alone we can do so little, together we can do so much." — Helen Keller

Security is mostly a superstition. It does not exist in nature, nor do the children of men as a whole experience it. Avoiding danger is no safer in the long run than outright exposure. Life is either a daring adventure or nothing." — Helen Keller

The only thing worse that being blind is having no vision." — Helen Keller

The best and most beautiful things in this world cannot be seen or even heard, but must be felt with the heart." — Helen Keller

A happy life consists not in the absence, but in the mastery of hardships." — Helen Keller

When you face the sun, the shadows always fall behind you." — Helen Keller

What I am looking for is not out there, it is in me." — Helen Keller

Howard Gardner

Few things could make a scholar more pleased than the discovery that someone has been able to effect a powerful relationship—and for that matter, a practical one—between two major lines of work, each of which he has pursued for decades." — Howard Gardner

I have come to realize that once one releases an idea—a "meme"—into the world, one cannot completely control its behavior, anymore than one can control those products of our genes called children." — Howard Gardner

Psychology does not directly dictate education; it merely helps one to understand the conditions within which education takes place." — Howard Gardner

It has become a truism that ours is an era devoid of heroes and bereft of leadership." — Howard Gardner

...the importance attached to the number is not entirely inappropriate: after all, the score on an intelligence test does predict one's ability to handle school subjects, though it foretells little of success in later life." — Howard Gardner

...it is not possible, and may not be appropriate, for the originator of a theory to attempt to control the ways in which it is used." — Howard Gardner

An intelligence is the ability to solve problems, or to create products, that are valued within one or more cultural settings." — Howard Gardner

Intelligence as an interaction between, on the one hand, certain proclivities and potentials and, on the other, the opportunities and constraints that characterize a particular cultural setting." — Howard Gardner

You don't need to light a candle in your home, walk around barefoot, or post a photo of yourself doing tree pose on a mountaintop. Becoming a monk is a mindset that anyone can adopt." — Jay Shetty

...we can't elevate to the monk mindset by digging down to the root of what we want and creating actionable steps for growth. The monk mindset lifts us out of confusion and distraction and helps us find clarity, meaning, and direction."
— Jay Shetty

When you try to live your most authentic life, some of your relationships will be put in jeopardy. Losing them is a risk worth bearing; finding a way to keep them in your life is a challenge worth taking on." — Jay Shetty

There are three routes to happiness, all of them centered on knowledge: learning, progressing and achieving." — Jay Shetty

The only thing that stays with you from the moment you are born until the moment you die is your breath. All your friends, your family, the country you live in, all of that can change. The only thing that stays with you is your breath." — Jay Shetty

When you try to live your most authentic life, some of your relationships will be put in jeopardy. Losing them is a risk worth bearing; finding a way to keep them in your life is a challenge worth taking on." — Jay Shetty

Society's definition of a happy life is anybody's and nobody's. The only way to build a meaningful life is to filter out that noise and look within. This is the first step to building your monk mind." — Jay Shetty

When we tune out the opinions, expectations, and obligations of the world around us, we begin to hear ourselves." — Jay Shetty

Every time you move homes or take a different job or embark on a new relationship, you have a golden opportunity to reinvent yourself." — Jay Shetty

It feels good to be around people who are good for us; it doesn't feel good to be around people who don't support us or bring out our bad habits." — Jay Shetty

We are social creatures who get most of what we want in life — peace, love and understanding — from the group we gather around us. Our brains adjust automatically to both harmony and disagreement." — Jay Shetty

In life, as in sports, being around better players pushes us to grow." — Jay Shetty

The more we define ourselves in relation to the people around us, the more lost we are." — Jay Shetty

We think freedom is being able to say whatever we want. We think freedom means that we can pursue all our desires. Real freedom is letting go of things not wanted, the unchecked desires that lead us to unwanted ends." — Jay Shetty

Revenge is the mode of ignorance—it is often said that you can't fix yourself by breaking someone else." — Jay Shetty

When we wrap our heads around the fact that we can't undo the past, we begin to accept our own imperfections and mistakes, forgive ourselves, and in doing so, open ourselves up to the emotional healing we all yearn for." — Jay Shetty

It's hard to find a comedy show that's not based on negative observations. But there is a line between negativity that helps us navigate life and negativity that puts more pain out into the world." — Jay Shetty

When you stop feeling so curious about others' misfortunes and instead take pleasure in their successes, you are healing." — Jay Shetty

The less time you fixate on everyone else, the more time you have to focus on yourself." — Jay Shetty

The longer we hold on to fears, the more they ferment until eventually they become toxic." — Jay Shetty

We transform hurtful fears into useful fears by focusing on what we can control. We can't stop our parents from dying, but we use the fear to remind us to spend more time with them." — Jay Shetty

Life is not a collection of unrelated events. It's a narrative that stretches into the past and the future." — Jay Shetty

When we learn to stop segmenting experiences and periods of our life and instead see them as scenes and acts in a larger

narrative, we gain perspective that help us deal with fear." —
Jay Shetty

Fear motivates us. Sometimes it motivates us toward what we want, but sometimes if we aren't careful, it limits us with what we think will keep us safe." — Jay Shetty

When we let achievements and acquisitions determine our course, we are living in the illusion that happiness comes from external measures of success, but all too often we find that when we finally get what we want, when we find success, it doesn't lead to happiness." — Jay Shetty

Our search is never for a thing, but for the feeling we think the thing will give us." — Jay Shetty

Happiness and fulfillment come only from mastering the mind and connecting with the soul—not from objects or attainments. Success doesn't guarantee happiness, and happiness doesn't require success." — Jay Shetty

Monks know that one can't plant a garden of beautiful flowers and leave it to thrive on its own. We have to be gardeners of our own lives, planting only the seeds of good intentions, watching to see what they become, and removing the weeds that spring up and get in the way." — Jay Shetty

Everyone has a psychophysical nature which determines where they flourish and thrive." — Jay Shetty

Our society is set up around strengthening our weaknesses rather than building our strength." — Jay Shetty

Play hardest in your area of strength and you will achieve depth, meaning, and satisfaction in your life." — Jay Shetty

Instead of making a huge career change, you can try my approach: look for opportunities to do what you love in the life you already have." — Jay Shetty

When we get in the habit of identifying what empowers us, we have a better understanding of ourselves and what we want in life." — Jay Shetty

Morning sets the tone of the day, but a well — planned evening prepares you for morning." — Jay Shetty

Life messes up your plans. Tomorrow is not going to go as you visualize it. Visualization doesn't change your life, but it changes how you see it." — Jay Shetty

People complain about their poor memories, but I have heard it said that we don't have a retention problem, we have an attention problem. By searching for the new, you are reminding your brain to pay attention and rewiring it to recognize that there's something to learn in everything. Life isn't as certain as we assume." — Jay Shetty

Change happens with small steps and big priorities. Pick one thing to change, make it your number one priority, and see it through before you move on to the next." — Jay Shetty

The ocean is full of treasures, but if you swim on the surface, you won't see them all." — Jay Shetty

All of us have a history of pain, heartbreak, and challenges, whatever they may be. Just because we have been through

something and it's safely in the past doesn't mean it's over."
— Jay Shetty

Just sharing a new word in conversation can bring rich to the dinner table." — Jay Shetty

Writing by itself doesn't solve all our problems, but it can help us gain critical perspectives we can use to find solutions." — Jay Shetty

Attachment brings pain. If you think something is yours or you think you are something, then it hurts to have it taken away from you." — Jay Shetty

You don't have to take vows or eat pine needles to explore your limits. Often all that holds us back from achieving the impossible is the belief that it is possible." — Jay Shetty

Though life remains imperfect, you accept it as it is and see a clear path ahead." — Jay Shetty

If you are satisfied with who you are, you don't need to prove your worth to anyone else." — Jay Shetty

In the act of criticizing others for failing to live up to higher standards, we ourselves are failing to live up to the highest standards." — Jay Shetty

When you presume knowledge, you put up a barrier that nothing can cross, and miss out on a potential learning opportunity." — Jay Shetty

If you inspire special treatment, it is because people appreciate you, but when you demand or feel entitled to it, you are looking for respect that you haven't heard." — Jay Shetty

You can only keep up the myth of your own importance for so long. If you don't break your ego, life will break it for you." — Jay Shetty

Some tasks build competence, and some build character." — Jay Shetty

Humility comes from accepting where you are without seeing it as a reflection of who you are." — Jay Shetty

If we can get past the idea that we'll break of everything doesn't go our way immediately, our capability expand exponentially." — Jay Shetty

Feedback often doesn't tell you which direction to follow, it just propels you on your way. You need to make your decisions and then take actions." — Jay Shetty

The measure of success isn t numbers, it's depth." — Jay Shetty

Real greatness is when you use your own achievements to teach others, and they learn how to teach others, and the greatness that you have accomplished expands exponentially." — Jay Shetty

The most powerful, admirable, captivating quality in any human is seen when they've achieved great things, but still embrace humility and their own significance." — Jay Shetty

In order to create something we have to imagine it. This is why visualization is so important. Whatever we build internally can be built externally." — Jay Shetty

We aren't careful with when and how we give our trust. We either trust other people too easily, we withhold our trust from everyone." — Jay Shetty

...someone's looks aren't who they are—the body is only a vessel for the soul." — Jay Shetty

If you don't know what you want, you will send out the wrong signals and attract the wrong people. If you aren't self—aware, you'll look for the wrong qualities and choose the wrong people." — Jay Shetty

Fresh experiences bring excitement into your life and build a stronger bond." — Jay Shetty

There is a difference between being grateful for what you have and settling for less than you deserved." — Jay Shetty

In every relationship you have the opportunity to set the level of joy you expect and the level of pain you will accept." — Jay Shetty

You may undervalue yourself in the moment of breakup, but your value doesn't depend on someone's ability to fully appreciate you." — Jay Shetty

If you have lost yourself in a relationship, find yourself in the heartbreak." — Jay Shetty

You can either see the world through the lens of love and duty, or through the lens of necessity and force. Love and duty are more likely to lead to happiness." — Jay Shetty

Life is not going to go your way. You have to go your way and take life with you. Understanding this will help you be prepared for whatever may come." — Jay Shetty

Jim Rohn

You must take personal responsibility. You cannot change the circumstance, the seasons or the wind, but you can change yourself." — Jim Rohn

Too much of everything — even good things — get you off track." — Jim Rohn

Don't let your learning lead to knowledge; let your learning lead to action." — Jim Rohn

You can't read too many books, but you can read too few." — Jim Rohn

Don't ask for security; ask for adventure." — Jim Rohn

It is not important how long you live. What is important is how you live." — Jim Rohn

Poor thinking habit makes most people poor." — Jim Rohn

Reading is essential for those who seek to rise above the ordinary." – Jim Rohn

Life was designed not to give us what we want or what we need. It was designed to give us what we deserve." – Jim Rohn

The ambitious person realised that each of us needs all of us." — Jim Rohn

If you don't design your own life plan, chances are you'll fall into someone else's plan. And guess what they have planned for you? Not much." — Jim Rohn

Life was designed not to give us what we want or what we need. It is design to give us what we deserve." — Jim Rohn

<u>Joe Biden</u>

History, faith and reason show the way, the way of unity. We can see each other not as adversaries, but as neighbors. We can treat each other with dignity and respect. We can join forces, stop the shouting and lower the temperature. For without unity, there is no peace — only bitterness and fury. No progress — only exhausting outrage. No nation — only a state of chaos." — Joe Biden

There's no accounting for what fate will deal you. Some days when you need a hand. There are other days when we're called to lend a hand. That's how it has to be. That's what we do for one another." — Joe Biden

America has been tested and we've come out stronger for it. We will repair our alliances and engage with the world once again. Not to meet yesterday's challenges, but today's and tomorrow's challenges. And we'll lead, not merely by the example of our power, but by the power of our example." — Joe Biden

Keep everything I do in your service, thinking not of power, but of possibilities, not of personal interest, but the public good." — Joe Biden

Politics doesn't have to be a raging fire, destroying everything in its path. Every disagreement doesn't have to be a cause for total war. And we must reject the culture in which facts themselves are manipulated and even manufactured." — Joe Biden

<u>Joel Osteen</u>

Dreams are just dreams without goals; they are ultimately a disappointment." — Joel Osteen

Don't complain about the pain, grow through the pain. Without the pain, you can't reach the fullness of your destiny." — Joel Osteen

Healing comes when you get your mind off your own pain, and you go help others." — Joel Osteen

God is not waiting for the conditions to be right before He blesses you. He made a river from the desert..." — Joel Osteen

The reasons the enemies are fighting you is because there is a calling for you, an assignment for your life." — Joel Osteen

The enemy makes his most noise when he is on his way out of your life." — Joel Osteen

When you fall down, don't stay down. You have to rise again." — Joel Osteen

Dreams are just dreams without goals; they are ultimately a disappointment."

Don't complain about the pain, grow through the pain. Without the pain, you can't reach the fullness of your destiny." — Joel Osteen

Healing comes when you get your mind off your own pain, and you go help others." — Joel Osteen

God makes us go through something so that we can be uniquely qualified and instrumental in assisting others and lift them in their time of need." — Joel Osteen

Life is too short to go through it with negative things to fill you through." — Joel Osteen

Worry will make you weak. Doubt will make you stressed out. Resentment will shortening your life." — Joel Osteen

It is easy to remorse when you have been overwhelmed by defeat or disappointment. But a simple way to turn that around is by declaring to remorseness that you have been strengthened than what it can poison." — Joel Osteen

Self—pity is like rising against yourself. And rising against yourself pushes you down." — Joel Osteen

Unforgiveness is like a poison to you. You may be feeling good with those grudges, but they are contaminating your life." — Joel Osteen

What you keep before your eyes will affect you. You will produce what you are continually seeing in your mind. If you foster an image of defeat and failure, then you are going to live that kind of life. But if you develop an image of victory, success, health, abundance, joy, peace, and happiness, nothing on earth will be able to hold those things from you." — Joel Osteen.

You cannot have a larger life with restricted attitudes. You must stop dwelling on negative, destructive thoughts that keeps you in a rut. Your life is not going to change until you change your thinking." — Joel Osteen.

Keep your mind moving in the right direction. You can't have a victim mentality and expect to live in victory." — Joel Osteen

The tragedy is, if we don't change our believing, we could go through our entire lifetimes missing out on the great things God has in store for us." — Joel Osteen

God ways are not our ways. They are higher and better than our ways. If you can see the invincible, God will do the impossible." — Joel Osteen

Life is a self—fulfilling prophecy." — Joel Osteen

Your circumstances don't have you down. Your thoughts about your circumstances have you down." — Joel Osteen

Our thoughts and expectations wield tremendous power and influence in our lives. We don't always get what we deserve in life, but we usually get no more than we expect; we receive what we believe." — Joel Osteen

Those who wait on the LORD shall renew their strength. In this life you will have trouble, but be of good cheer for I have overcome the world." — Joel Osteen

As a person think in his heart, so he will become." — Joel Osteen

We can all sit back and make excuses to have an attitude, to have a poor self—image. Anyone can do that. But if we want to live in victory, we need to shake off self—pity and move on with our lives." — Joel Osteen

People who harbor anger don't realise it, but they are poisoning their own lives. When we don't forgive, we are not hurting the other person. We are not hurting the company that did us wrong. We are not hurting God. We are only hurting ourselves." — Joel Osteen

If you don't have a vision for it, it's not going to happen. Without a vision you won't see God's best. You won't be the winner He wants you to be." — Joel Osteen

The problem is you're being limited by your own imagination. You've got to change what you're seeing. Don't let negative thoughts paint those pictures. Use your imagination to see yourself accomplishing dreams, rising higher, overcoming obstacles, being healthy, strong, blessed, and prosperous." — Joel Osteen.

This is a new day; things are changing in your favor. Hold your head up high. What's in front of you is much greater than what is behind you." — Joel Osteen.

Successful people don't waste their time looking at what everybody else is doing. They're too busy focusing on what God has put in their heart." — Joel Osteen.

If you can accomplish your dreams in your own strength, talent, ability, and resources, then your dreams are too small. You don't need God's help with small dreams. Believe big. Your destiny is too great, your assignment too important, to have little goals, little dreams, little prayers." — Joel Osteen

We should stop emphasizing what is wrong and start thanking God for what is right." — Joel Osteen

If you don't learn how to be contended with where you are, you are never going to get to where you want to be." — Joel Osteen

God doesn't bless mediocrity. He blesses excellence and integrity." — Joel Osteen

Integrity is the foundation on which any successful life is built." — Joel Osteen.

Instead of judging people, why don't you take that same time to pray for them, to reach out to them, to let them know that you believe in them." — Joel Osteen

It's very freeing when you realize you don't have to prove anything. Some of the people you're trying to outperform, they're not even watching." — Joel Osteen

Don't give away your power. Don't put your identity, your value in someone else's hands." — Joel Osteen

Gratefulness is an expression of faith. It says, "I'm looking at the future, not at the past." — Joel Osteen

Don't worry about being in the right group, having the most friends, being the most popular. It's not the quantity of friends that's important; it's the quality of your friends." — Joel Osteen

The people that succeed don't always have the most talent, the most education, the most opportunity. Many times, they simply want it more. I want to light a fire in you today. You have to go after what God has for you." — Joel Osteen

You have to give people the grace to change. Don't judge their whole life on one season, one mistake." — Joel Osteen

If you're going to see what you're believing for, you have to be willing to do what other people won't do. Don't miss your destiny because you didn't want it bad enough." — Joel Osteen

God sees potential in you that you can't see in yourself. He's going to present you with opportunities that seem way over your head. Don't shrink back. You are well able." — Joel Osteen

Start the day with a positive thought. Always begin your day with a positive thought about what's in store for you and about yourself. This sets the tone for the day ahead. Don't be scared to compliment yourself – the key here is to raise your vibration so that you can attract more positive events throughout the day and generally feel good!" — Joel Osteen

Life is like a car; you have a forward gear and a reverse gear. You decide which way you want to go. It doesn't take any more effort to go forward than it does backward." — Joel Osteen

The real battle takes place in your mind. What are you dwelling on all day? That's what you're attracting. Sometimes your body will not get well until your mind tells it to get well." — Joel Osteen

God rewards excellence. When you do more than what's required, you will see God's goodness in new ways. Whether you have much or a little, whether it's old or new, take pride in what God has given you." — Joel Osteen

God did not create us to reach one level and then stop. Whether you're nine or ninety years old, you should constantly be learning, improving your skills, and getting better at what you do." — Joel Osteen

I read that the wealthiest places on earth are not the oil fields of the Middle East or the diamond mines of South Africa. The wealthiest places are the cemeteries. Buried in the ground are businesses that were never formed, books that were never written, songs that were never sung, dreams that never came to life, potential that was never released." — Joel Osteen

Positive people have made up their minds to enjoy life. They focus on the possibility, not the problem. They're grateful for what they have, and they don't complain about what they don't have. Positive people know that God is in control, and that nothing happens without His permission. They choose to bloom where they are planted. They're not waiting to be happy when the situation changes. They're happy while God is changing the situation." — Joel Osteen

If you don't learn what you're supposed to learn along the way, you won't be able to handle where God is taking you." — Joel Osteen

John C. Maxwell

Your attitude, more than your aptitude, will determine your altitude." — John C. Maxwell

A problem is something that can be solved. A fact of life is something that must be accepted." — John C. Maxwell

People say there are two kinds of learning: experience, which is gained from your own mistakes, and wisdom, which is learned from the mistakes of others." — John C. Maxwell

Most people are capable of making a living. The significant thing is making a difference." — John C. Maxwell

You don't have to love change to be successful, but you need to be willing to accept it. Change is a catalyst for personal growth. It gets you out of a rut, it gives you a fresh start, and it affords you an opportunity to reevaluate your direction. If you resist change, you're really resisting success. Learn flexibility, or learn to like living with your failures." — John C. Maxwell

If you want to grow and become the best person you can be, you've got to be intentional about it." — John C. Maxwell

Growth must be intentional—nobody improves by accident." — John C. Maxwell

As a leader, the first person I need to lead is myself." — John C. Maxwell

If you want to succeed as a mentor, first seek to understand yourself and others." — John C. Maxwell

The only way to improve the quality of your life is to improve yourself." — John C. Maxwell

Most people don't realize that unsuccessful and successful people do not differ substantially in their abilities. They vary in their desires to reach their potential. And nothing is more effective when it comes to reaching potential than commitment to personal growth." — John C. Maxwell

No matter where you may be starting from, don't be discouraged; everyone who got where he is started where he was." — John C. Maxwell

The will to win is a waste if you do not have the will to prepare." — John C. Maxwell

You can be young only once, but you can be immature indefinitely." — John C. Maxwell

If your life doesn't begin to change as a result of what you're learning, you're experiencing one of these problems: You're not giving your growth plan enough time and attention; you're focusing too much time on the wrong areas; or you're not applying what you learn." — John C. Maxwell

Growth is always worth the price you pay because the alternative is a limited life with unfulfilled potential." — John C. Maxwell

A true calling is never about the person being called. It's about helping others. A calling moves us from the center of everything in our world to becoming the channel through which good things come to others." — John C. Maxwell

Your calling will result in the merging of your skills, talents, character traits, and experiences. It will make use of your experience, your gifts, and the lessons you've learned. It will be represented by a deep desire to create, lead, inspire, and make a difference." — John C. Maxwell

The road to the next level is uphill, and it takes effort to keep growing. The sooner you start, the closer to reaching your potential you'll be." — John C. Maxwell

Talent is a gift but character is a choice." — John C. Maxwell

To add value to others, one must first value others." — John C. Maxwell

Messages that give us feedback about life. Interruptions that should cause us to reflect and think. Signposts that direct us to the right path. Tests that push us toward greater maturity. Awakenings that keep us in the game mentally. Keys that we can use to unlock the next door of opportunity. Explorations that let us journey where we've never been before. Statements about our development and progress." — John C. Maxwell

Contentment comes from having a positive attitude. It means: expecting the best in everything—not the worst; remaining upbeat—even when you get beat up; seeing solutions in every problem—not problems in every solution; believing in yourself—even when others believe you've failed and holding on to hope—even when others say it's hopeless." — John C. Maxwell

Your network determines your net worth." — John C. Maxwell

You can't let the failure outside you get inside you. You certainly can't control the length of your life—but you can control its width and depth. You can't control the contour of your face—but you can control its expression. You can't control the weather—but you can control the atmosphere of your mind. Why worry about things you can't control when you can keep yourself busy controlling the things that depend on you?" — John C. Maxwell

The difference between average people and achieving people is their perception of and response to failure." — John C. Maxwell

The ability to learn from mistakes has value not just in business, but in all aspects of life. If you live to learn, then you will really learn to live." — John C. Maxwell

No matter how difficult your problems were, the key to overcoming them doesn't lie in changing your circumstances. It's in changing yourself." — John C. Maxwell

One of the greatest problems people have with failure is that they are too quick to judge isolated situations in their lives and label them as failures. Instead, they need to keep the bigger picture in mind." — John C. Maxwell

Success is not a destination — not a place where you arrive one day. Instead, it is the journey you take. And whether you succeed comes from what you do day to day." — John C. Maxwell

You are the only person who can really label what you do a failure. It's subjective. Your perception of and response to your mistakes determine whether your actions are failures." — John C. Maxwell

All great achievers are given multiple reasons to believe they are failures. But in spite of that, they persevere." — John C. Maxwell

People who see failure as the enemy are captives to those who conquer it." — John C. Maxwell

Errors become mistakes when we perceive them and respond to them incorrectly. Mistakes become failures when we continually respond to them incorrectly." — John C. Maxwell

Every fulfilled dream occurred because of dedication to a process." — John C. Maxwell

Many people who struggle with chronic failure do so because they think of no one but themselves." — John C. Maxwell

The problems of people's pasts impact them in one of two ways: They experience either a breakdown or a breakthrough." — John C. Maxwell

Risk must be evaluated not by the fear it generates in you or the probability of your success, but by the value of the goal." — John C. Maxwell

Leadership is not about position, title or flowchart. It's about one life influencing another." — John C. Maxwell

Every major difficulty you face in life is a fork in the road. You choose which track you will head down, toward breakdown or breakthrough." — John C. Maxwell

When you get better, it makes you bigger. Growth is sustaining. Growth is the only guarantee that tomorrow will be better than today." — John C. Maxwell

No successful person has ever experienced accidental achievements. Nothing of genuine value is easy, quick, and downhill. If we want to succeed in leadership, we must do what we don't want to do, so we can do what we need to do. We must be willing to pay the price." — John C. Maxwell

The ability to innovate is at the heart of creativity — a vital component in success." — John C. Maxwell

If you want to succeed, you have to learn to make adjustments to the way you do things and try again." — John C. Maxwell

More than anything else, what keeps a person going in the midst of adversity is having a sense of purpose. It is the fuel that powers persistence." — John C. Maxwell

People who personalize failure see a problem as a hole they're permanently stuck in. But achievers see any predicament as temporary." — John C. Maxwell

If your people need motivating, then you have the wrong people. Motivation is an inside job — it starts within each person and comes in an infinite variety. If you as leader have to work through the combinations to find the exact right motivation for each person on your team, you'll never get anything done. Instead, it's better for your people to motivate themselves and for you as their leader to inspire them." — John C. Maxwell

Dream is an inspiring picture of the future that energizes your mind, will, and emotions, empowering you to do everything you can to achieve it." — John C. Maxwell

Competence is a key to credibility, and credibility is the key to influencing others. If people respect you, they will listen to you." — John C. Maxwell

You can't change the world by giving only leftovers or by performing with mediocrity. Only your best will add value to others and lift them up." — John C. Maxwell

The more specific you can get about your strengths, the better the chance you can find your "sweet spot." — John C. Maxwell

Being a good listener helps us to know people better, to learn what they have learned, and to show them that we value them as individuals." — John C. Maxwell

Dreams come true when gifts are set on fire with passion. The best career advice you will ever receive is to discover your passion and follow it. When you make your dream your profession, you experience fulfillment most of the days of your life." — John C. Maxwell

The bigger the dream, the bigger the person you must become to achieve it." — John C. Maxwell

When achievers fail, they see it as a momentary event, not a lifelong epidemic." — John C. Maxwell

"To succeed in life, we must stay within our strength zone but continually move outside our comfort zone". — John C. Maxwell.

People don't need to follow the common path to be successful." — John C. Maxwell

The best leaders are characterized by the ability to recognize the special abilities and limitations of others, and the capacity to fit their people into the jobs where they will do best." — John C. Maxwell

Adversity lies in every success." — John C. Maxwell

Experience teaches nothing, but evaluated experience teaches everything." — John C. Maxwell

The average person makes a mistake and automatically thinks that it's a failure. But some of the greatest stories of success can be found in the unexpected benefits of mistakes." — John C. Maxwell

There is nothing noble in being superior to someone else, progress is becoming superior to your previous self." — John C. Maxwell

<u>Kobe Bryant</u>

I have nothing in common with lazy people who blame others for their lack of success. Great things come from hard work and perseverance. No excuses." — Kobe Bryant

It's not about the number of hours you practice, it's about the number of hours your mind is present during the practice." — Kobe Bryant

When the game is more important than the injury, you won't feel the injury." — Kobe Bryant

If you want to be great in a particular area, you have to obsess over it. A lot of people say they want to be great, but they're not willing to make the sacrifices necessary to achieve greatness. They have other concerns, whether important or not, and they spread themselves out." — Kobe Bryant

I remain focused on changing the world in positive ways through diverse stories, characters and leadership in order to inspire the next generation." — Kobe Bryant

Everything negative — pressure, challenges - is all an opportunity for me to rise." — Kobe Bryant

I like challenging people and making them uncomfortable. That's what leads to introspection and that's what leads to improvement. You could say I dared people to be their best selves." — Kobe Bryant

Les Brown

You can't be allowing your emotions to control you. If you are being control by your emotions, they will use you." — Les Brown

Sometimes, you just have to look for someone you can help so that you can forget yourself." — Les Brown

Life is not going to give you what you want, it will give you what you are." — Les Brown

The difference between eyesight and mind—sight is that eyesight is about using your eyes what you see (appearance); while mind—sight is about using your mind to interpret what you see." — Les Brown

You have to do what you can, where you are with what you have." — Les Brown

You will go through things that you wouldn't understand why such things are happening to you. But when it is time for you to use your experience, you will appreciate your lessons." — Les Brown

An uncommitted life doesn't worth living. Why? Because it wouldn't produce anything!" — Les Brown

If you want to be good at something, you must study the people who have mastered it." — Les Brown

The universe respond to man or woman that refuses to be denied." — Les Brown

Commitment takes a stand for you: It means delivery, it means breaking through. Why won't you commit yourself towards something in your life?" — Les Brown

It is either they adjust to your pace, or you adjust to their pace." — Les Brown

Don't go out there and be telling people to watch your story. Eighty percent don't care, while it is only twenty percent that care that it is you." — Les Brown

The more you give to life, the more you get from it." — Les Brown

If you don't act on life, life will act on you." — Les Brown

The truth is, everybody dies, but not everybody lives." — Les Brown

You are a masterpiece because you are a piece of the Master." — Les Brown

Always shoot for the moon; even, if you missed your target, you will hit the stars." — Les Brown

Life is like a onion, you have to peel it one layer at a time and sometime, you have to cry." — Les Brown

To get something you never had, you have to do something you never did." — Les Brown

You have to use what you have. Not how much you have." — Les Brown

Sometime, it is better to figure out where you are going because your life will never be on a straight path." — Les Brown

One of the most powerful assets that could ever be released by any man is that drive to believe that all will be well regardless of what he had been through." — Les Brown

In order for you to have a tomorrow you don't have today, you have to do what you don't do yesterday today." — Les Brown

I can afford to give anything. You can't afford to give nothing." — Les Brown

There are unnecessary losses we encounter in life, which are results of what we don't do because we want people to like us." — Les Brown

Success is doing what you love to do and in finding someone to be paying you for it." — Les Brown

Stand up for what you believe because you can fall for anything." — Les Brown

In my own opinion, I don't believe necessity is the mother of invention. The mother of invention is refusing to accept things as they are." — Les Brown

If you don't program yourself, life will program you." — Les Brown

Using the word "but" means you wants to be giving excuses to validate your inactions." — Les Brown

If you don't have a goal for being here, then being here doesn't worth it." — Les Brown

It is what you do that will indicate if you are either a prospect or suspect." — Les Brown

Most people fail in life not just because they aim too high, but because they aim too low." — Les Brown

Sometimes the only good things you will hear about you are the ones you say to yourself." — Les brown

It is not what you leave for your children; it is what you leave in them." — Les Brown

If you are too casual with your dream, you will end up being a casualty." — Les Brown

Your speaking is a projection of whom you are, not who you think you ought to be." — Les Brown

I want you to believe that it all lies within us, something that speaks about our purpose and pushes us to our responsibility." — Les Brown

People that are hungry are willing to do what others don't do." — Les Brown

Life is all about fighting for your territory. When you stop fighting for what you want, what you don't want will take over." — Les Brown

In life, you may not get everything you have fight for. But whatever you get is a reward for your fights." — Les Brown

Mahatma Gandhi

In a gentle way, you can shake the world." — Mahatma Gandhi

The history of the world is full of men who rose to leadership, by sheer force of self—confidence, bravery, and tenacity." – Mahatma Gandhi

The only devils in the world are those running in our own hearts. That is where the battle should be fought." — Mahatma Gandhi

If we could change ourselves, the tendencies in the world would also change. As a man changes his own nature, so does the attitude of the world change towards him." — Mahatma Gandhi

Freedom is not worth having if it does not include the freedom to make mistakes." — Mahatma Gandhi

If I have the belief that I can do it, I shall surely acquire the capacity to do it, even if I do not have it at the beginning." — Mahatma Gandhi

The best way to find yourself is to lose yourself in the service of others." — Mahatma Gandhi

The difference between what we do and what we are capable of doing would suffice to solve most of the world's problems." — Mahatma Gandhi

The world has enough for everyone's need, but not enough for everyone's greed." — Mahatma Gandhi

<u>Mao Ming</u>

In the world today, changes unseen in a century are accelerating, and the force for peace, development and progress has continued to grow. It falls upon us to follow the prevailing trend of history, and choose cooperation over confrontation, openness over seclusion, and mutual benefit over zero—sum games. We shall be firm in opposing all forms of hegemony and power politics, as well as all forms of unilateralism and protectionism." — Mao Ming

We should vigorously advocate peace, development, equity, justice, democracy and freedom, which are the common values of humanity, and work together to provide the right guiding philosophy for building a better world. Peace and development are our common cause, equity and justice our common aspiration, and democracy and freedom our common pursuit." — Mao Ming

Diversity makes human civilisation what it is, and provides a constant source of vitality and driving force for world development. No civilisation in the world is superior to others; every civilisation is special and unique to its own region." — Mao Ming

Civilisations can achieve harmony only through communication, and can make progress only through harmonisation. Whether a country's path of development works is judged, first and foremost, by whether it fits the country's conditions; whether it follows the development trend of the times; whether it brings about economic growth, social advancement, better livelihoods and social stability;

whether it has the people's endorsement and support; and whether it contributes to the progressive cause of humanity." — Mao Ming

Humanity should overcome difficulties in solidarity and pursue common development in harmony. To build a community with a shared future for mankind is not to replace one system or civilisation with another. Instead, it is about countries with different social systems, ideologies, histories, cultures and levels of development coming together for shared interests, shared rights and shared responsibilities in global affairs, and creating the greatest synergy for building a better world." — Mao Ming

Development is meaningful only when it is for the people's interest, and can sustain only when it is motivated by the people. Countries should put their people front and centre, and strive to realise development with a higher level of quality, efficiency, equity, sustainability and security." — Mao Ming

Mark Twain

Keep away from people who try to belittle your ambitions. Small people always do that, but the really great make you feel that you, too, can become great. When you are seeking to bring big plans to fruition, it is important with whom you regularly associate." — Mark Twain

With courage, you will dare to take risks, have the strength to be compassionate, and the wisdom to be humble. Courage is the foundation of integrity." - Mark Twain

The secret of getting ahead is getting started. The secret of getting started is breaking your overwhelming complex tasks into small manageable tasks and then starting with the first one." — Mark Twain

I know a man who grabbed a cat by the tail and he learned 40 percent more about cats than the man who didn't." — Mark Twain

Don't let schooling interfere with your education." — Mark Twain

It is not the size of the dog in the fight, it is the size of the fight in the dog." — Mark Twain

The worst loneliness is to not be comfortable with yourself." — Mark Twain

Forgiveness is the fragrance the violet sheds on the heel that has crushed it." — Mark Twain

Never put off till tomorrow what you can do after tomorrow."
— Mark Twain

The secret of getting ahead is getting started." – Mark Twain

In the beginning of a change, the patriot is a scarce man, and brave and hated and scorned. When the cause succeeds, the timid join him, for them it costs nothing to be a patriot." — Mark Twain

A man cannot be comfortable without his own approval." — Mark Twain

<u>Mark Zuckerberg</u>

I want to tell you that finding your purpose is not enough, what I am here to tell you tonight is that the major challenge of this generation is finding our sense of purpose." — Mark Zuckerberg

I was excited to connect Harvard community. But someday, someone will connect the whole world." — Mark Zuckerberg

Let's get things done for not just to create progress, but to create purpose." — Mark Zuckerberg

The greatest successes come from having the freedom to fail." — Mark Zuckerberg

My goal for this next decade isn't to be liked, but to be understood. In order to be trusted, people need to know what you stand for." — Mark Zuckerberg

<u>**Martin Luther King Jr.**</u>

We are not out to defeat or humiliate the white man but to free our children from a life of permanent psychological death." — Martin Luther King Jr.

We must accept finite disappointment, but we must never lose infinite hope." — Martin Luther King Jr.

The change we want is not rolled in the wheels of inevitability, but in continuous struggles." — Martin Luther King Jr.

Not everyone can be famous, but everyone can be great. And greatness is only achieved through service." — Martin Luther King Jr.

The coming together of every slave is the beginning of an end to slavery." — Martin Luther King Jr.

The ark of the moral universe may be long; but it bends toward justice." — Martin Luther King Jr.

You cannot keep birds from flying over your head but you can keep them from building a nest in your hair." — Martin Luther King Jr.

Be careful not to measure your holiness by other people's sins." — Martin Luther King Jr.

History will have to record that the greatest tragedy of this period of social transition was not the vociferous and discordant clamor of the bad people, but the appalling silent of the good people." — Martin Luther King Jr.

I am a believer in nonviolence. But I also believe that conscience is an open wound." — Martin Luther King Jr.

<u>Mohammed bin Rashid Al—Maktoun</u>

I am a believer that all our actions and accomplishments are simply a reflection of what we bear in our hearts." — Mohammed bin Rashid Al—Maktoun

A positive person is confident that no challenge will stand in the way of achieving his or her goal." — Mohammed bin Rashid Al—Maktoun

It is our mind and your way of thinking that create your reality. You choose whether you want to live your life with positive or negative energy." — Mohammed bin Rashid Al—Maktoun

An army's success depends on more than success and supplies; high morale can be a key to victory, just as low morale can spell defeat." — Mohammed bin Rashid Al—Maktoun

Creativity should be integral to everything that we do. Creativity should also be intrinsic to our personality, if excellence is what we seek." — Mohammed bin Rashid Al—Maktoun

Creativity is inherent in a person's make—up and way of thinking. To be creative is to add something new to life as opposed to being a passive part of it. We may not live for hundreds of years, but the products of our creativity can leave a legacy long after we have gone." — Mohammed bin Rashid Al—Maktoun

The future is for those who dare to dream and find the courage to pursue their dreams." — Mohammed bin Rashid Al—Maktoun

My advice to any leader, whether of a country, a company, a team or anything else, is to unite hearts before uniting efforts, and to feel the spirit before building the place." — Mohammed bin Rashid Al—Maktoun

We are no less than number one. Whoever convinces himself that he is not worthy of first position has doomed himself to failure from the very beginning." — Mohammed bin Rashid Al—Maktoun

Set a high goal for yourself and do not settle for anything less than the very best. The best is exactly what you will get if you accept no less." — Mohammed bin Rashid Al—Maktoun

We recognize the greatness of women, both at work and at home. A woman who raises great leaders is herself a great leader. Women have great capacity for generosity, giving and compassion." — Mohammed bin Rashid Al—Maktoun

Look at the history of the Arabs — we have recorded and passed on our stories in the form of poetry, and we have found that stories told in verse are deemed more sincere and more trustworthy than mere prose." — Mohammed bin Rashid Al—Maktoun

Every leader should have a passion in life that adds depth, uniqueness and style to his leadership." — Mohammed bin Rashid Al—Maktoun

My first advice is to acquire knowledge. You should surpass others in knowledge, for knowledge is the shortest path to victory, even in sports." — Mohammed bin Rashid Al—Maktoun

Training opens your eyes to your weaknesses, boosts your self—confidence and brings you a step closer to victory." — Mohammed bin Rashid Al—Maktoun

A true leader is one who forges great leaders." — Mohammed bin Rashid Al—Maktoun

Time is like a flowing river; you cannot step in the same water twice. One of my principles in life is that every minute of our life is worth filling with accomplishments, happiness and good deeds." — Mohammed bin Rashid Al—Maktoun

Some see the year as equivalent to 365 days. Well, I say that a year is equal to the number of days that you have invested in yourself, your family, your society or in your spiritual life." — Mohammed bin Rashid Al—Maktoun

The fresh thinking that fuels constant progress in government doesn't come from only the centre and the top, but from all around and from the roots." - Mohammed bin Rashid Al—Maktoun

People are not usually fond of change and tend to fight those who call for it, because it requires them to change their habits." — Mohammed bin Rashid Al—Maktoun

To all creative minds, I say: you will always find someone who will fight your ideas. This will be the first indication that you are on the right track. To all officials, I say: do not fight change — embrace it." — Mohammed bin Rashid Al—Maktoun

One of the most important lessons from both ancient and contemporary history is that the progress of countries, people and civilization started with education. The future of nations starts in their schools." — Mohammed bin Rashid Al—Maktoun

Improving education is a constant process that has no finish line, because the world is evolving." — Mohammed bin Rashid Al—Maktoun

Our region and its people are in dire need of a successful model in the Arab world — one that gives them hope and proves that focusing on growth is far better than focusing on wars; that launching projects is far more useful than launching rockets; and that building the future is only possible by consensus, reconciliation and team spirit." — Mohammed bin Rashid Al—Maktoun

Every nation can harness the energy of its citizens, either towards constructive work to generate optimism and hope, or towards tensions, unrest and war." — Mohammed bin Rashid Al—Maktoun

A person who does not take risks in life will avoid difficulties, problems and loss; but he will never mature or learn new things. He will never change." — Mohammed bin Rashid Al—Maktoun

To take risks and fail is not a failure. Real failure is to fear taking any risk." — Mohammed bin Rashid Al—Maktoun

Great men are defined by the challenges they take up. I personally cannot judge an individual's strength and capability, unless I confront him with a challenge. For challenges bring out a person's best and worst sides." — Mohammed bin Rashid Al—Maktoun

Every challenge is an opportunity for learning, a chance to test our capabilities and knowledge as well as the character of the people around us. Without challenges, victories and achievements would be meaningless." — Mohammed bin Rashid Al—Maktoun

True experience is measured not by the number of years that we have worked, but the number of challenges that we have taken up." — Mohammed bin Rashid Al—Maktoun

An easy life does not make men, nor does it build nations. Challenges make men, and it is these men who build nations.

I would like to tell you that impossible cannot be where there is perseverance and faith. There is no impossible in life." — Mohammed bin Rashid Al—Maktoun

Competition always makes you stronger and better. Competition is feared only by the weak." — Mohammed bin Rashid Al—Maktoun

The future belongs to those who generate ideas." — Mohammed bin Rashid Al—Maktoun

To err is human and we all fall short in our work sometimes; but the most important thing is not to be negligent or make errors on purpose." — Mohammed bin Rashid Al—Maktoun

A few mistakes made by a person working productively cost far less than a person paralysed by laziness or fear." — Mohammed bin Rashid Al—Maktoun

Success is not a destination, but a journey. Each time that you reach a summit on this journey, you must look ahead to the next one." — Mohammed bin Rashid Al—Maktoun

Government employees are the main drivers of development. They are our true capital. We count on them for improving our services, achieving our vision, and delivering on the expectations of our people." — Mohammed bin Rashid Al—Maktoun

Act like a leader, for true leadership is not in one's position, but in one's way of thinking and acting: it is in the mobility of one's objectives and goals." — Mohammed bin Rashid Al—Maktoun

A true leader does not derive power from his position, but from his ethics, from people's love for him, and from his knowledge, education and excellence in his field of work." — Mohammed bin Rashid Al—Maktoun

A true leader is one who creates a favourable environment to bring out the energy and ability of his team." — Mohammed bin Rashid Al—Maktoun

...for one's job is a major part of one's life, and life is too precious to spend in misery." — Mohammed bin Rashid Al—Maktoun

The future does not wait for hesitant people. The more we achieve, the more we realize how much more we can achieve." — Mohammed bin Rashid Al—Maktoun

A successful nation forges its own path to success without relying on the situation around it. A successful nation does not wait for the future, but rolls up its sleeves and make the future." — Mohammed bin Rashid Al—Maktoun

Anyone who can serve people and make them happy is a leader. A leader is also a person capable of creating positive change, whether at work or at home, and of innovating and creating even the simplest things. A leader excels in his craft, art, talent or profession." — Mohammed bin Rashid Al—Maktoun

All people are born with the seed of leadership, which they can nurture and grow, so that bit by bit, they advance on the path to leadership and ultimately evolve into great leaders." — Mohammed bin Rashid Al—Maktoun

A great vision needs not only a great leader, but also a great team with diverse leadership qualities." — Mohammed bin Rashid Al—Maktoun

Make time in your life for exercise, for this is the soundest investment that can be made in health, future and happiness." — Mohammed bin Rashid Al—Maktoun

Wealth does not come from your job; it comes from your personal gifting." — Myles Munroe

When purpose is not known, abuse is inevitable." — Myles Munroe

When you discover your gift, you find your arena of authority in life." — Myles Munroe

Wealth is given to fulfill purpose and divine assignment. You were not born to make a living but to make a difference." — Myles Munroe

When you discover your gift, you find your area of authority." — Myles Monroe

<u>Napoleon Hills</u>

Effort only fully releases its reward after a person refuses to quit." — Napoleon Hill

Every negative event contains the seed of an equal or greater benefit." — Napoleon Hill

History is filled with evidences that leadership by force cannot endure." — Napoleon Hill

If a leader is a REAL LEADER, he will have no need to advertise that fact except by his conduct—his sympathy, understanding, fairness, and a demonstration that he knows his job." — Napoleon Hill

It's not what you are going to do, but it's what you are doing now that counts." — Napoleon Hill

You can't change where you started, but you can change the direction you are going. It's not what you are going to do, but it's what you are doing now that counts." — Napoleon Hill

Cherish your visions and dreams, as they are the children of your soul, the blueprint of your ultimate achievements." — Napoleon Hill

The competent leader requires no "title" to give him the respect of his followers." — Napoleon Hill

If your imagination leads you to understand how quickly people grant your requests when those requests appeal to their self—interest, you can have practically anything you go after." - Napoleon Hill

More gold has been mined from the thoughts of man than has ever been taken from the earth." — Napoleon Hill

We see men who have accumulated great fortunes, but we often recognize on their triumphs, overlooking their temporary defeats which they had surmounted before arriving." — Napoleon Hill

<u>**Nelson Mandela**</u>

A freedom fighter learns the hard way that it is the oppressor who defines the nature of the struggle, and the oppressed is often left no recourse but to use methods that mirror those of the oppressor. At a certain point, one can only fight fire with fire." — Nelson Mandela

I never lose. I either win or learn." — Nelson Mandela

It is what we make of what we have, not what we are given, that separates one person from another." — Nelson Mandela

I am not extraordinary because I became the President of South Africa; I became extraordinary because I went through extraordinary circumstances." — Nelson Mandela

A leadership commits a crime against its own people if it hesitates to sharpen its political weapons where they have become less effective." — Nelson Mandela

The mentality of retaliation destroys states, while the mentality of tolerance builds nations. Also, to walk out of prison a free man is one thing. To gain that freedom, yet remain a prisoner of one's mind by refusing to forgive one's jailers is quite another." — Nelson Mandela

As a leader, one often seeks prominence; as an outlaw, the opposite is true." — Nelson Mandela

We have often said that our morality doesn't allow us to desert our friends." — Nelson Mandela

It is always the oppressor, not the oppressed, who dictates the form of the struggle. If the oppressor uses violence, the oppressed have no alternative but to respond violently." — Nelson Mandela

Life is not about not falling at all, but in rising every time you fall." — Nelson Mandela

A man does not become a freedom fighter in the hope of winning awards..." — Nelson Mandela

To make peace with an enemy one must work with that enemy, and that enemy becomes one's partner." — Nelson Mandela

Courage was not the absence of fear, but the triumph over it." — Nelson Mandela

Man's goodness is a flame that can be hidden but never extinguished." — Nelson Mandela

In life, every man has twin obligations — obligations to his family to his parents, to his wife and children; and he has an obligation to his people, his community, his country. In a civil and humane society, each man is able to fulfill those obligations according to his own inclinations and abilities." — Nelson Mandela

Freedom is indivisible; the chains on any one of my people were the chains on all of them, the chains on all of my people were the chains on me." — Nelson Mandela

I am not truly free if I am taking away someone else's freedom, just as surely as I am not free when my freedom is taken from me." — Nelson Mandela

For to be free is not merely to cast off one's chains, but to live in a way that respects and enhances the freedom of others." — Nelson Mandela

I have discovered the secret that after climbing a great hill, one only finds that there are many more hills to climb." — Nelson Mandela

The brave man is not he who does not feel afraid, but he who conquers that fear." — Nelson Mandela

Life will not change dramatically, except that you will have increased your self—esteem and become a citizen in your own land. You must have patience. You might have to wait five years for results to show." — Nelson Mandela

Which man of honour will desert a lifelong friend at the insistence of a common opponent and still retain a measure of credibility with his people?" — Nelson Mandela

Any house in which a man is free is a castle when compared to even the plushest prison." — Nelson Mandela

Freedom without civility, freedom without the ability to live in peace, was not true freedom at all." — Nelson Mandela

...we could not defeat the government on the battlefield, but could make governing difficult for them." — Nelson Mandela

Like the gardener, a leader must take responsibility for what he cultivates; he must mind his work, try to repel enemies, preserve what can be preserved, and eliminate what cannot succeed." — Nelson Mandela

I am not extraordinary because I am the president of South Africa; I became extraordinary because I went through extraordinary circumstances." — Nelson Mandela

Education is the most powerful weapon you can use to transform the world." — Nelson Mandela

The wife of a freedom fighter is often like a widow, even when her husband is not in prison." — Nelson Mandela

If the majority of the organization or the people support a decision, coercion can be used in certain cases against the dissident minority in the interests of the majority. A minority, however vocal, should not be able to frustrate the will of the majority." — Nelson Mandela

No one truly knows a nation until one has been inside its jails. A nation should not be judged by how it treats its highest citizens, but its lowest ones." — Nelson Mandela

...for a revolution is not just a question of pulling a trigger; its purpose is to create a fair and just society." — Nelson Mandela

I have found that one can bear the unbearable if one can keep one's spirits strong even when one's body is being tested. Strong convictions are the secret of surviving deprivation; your spirit can be full even when your stomach is empty." — Nelson Mandela

It is one thing to be told of possible hardships ahead, it is entirely another to actually have to confront them." — Nelson Mandela

It is important for a freedom fighter to remain in touch with his own roots, and the hurly—burly of city life has a way of erasing the past." — Nelson Mandela

Politics can be strengthened by music, but music has a potency that defies politics." — Nelson Mandela

The mentality of retaliation destroys states, while the mentality of tolerance builds nations. Also, to walk out of prison a free man is one thing. To gain that freedom, yet remain a prisoner of one's mind by refusing to forgive one's jailers is quite another." — Nelson Mandela

I would say that the whole life of any thinking African in this country drives him continuously to a conflict between his conscience on the one hand and the law on the other." — Nelson Mandela

A mother's death causes a man to look back on and evaluate his own life." — Nelson Mandela

To truly lead one's people one must also truly know them." — Nelson Mandela

A hero was a man who would not break even under the most trying circumstances." — Nelson Mandela

For to men, freedom in their own land is the pinnacle of their ambitions, from which nothing can turn men of conviction aside." — Nelson Mandela

Nothing is more dehumanizing than the absence of human companionship." — Nelson Mandela

...there is nothing as dangerous as a leader making a demand that he knows cannot be achieved. It creates false hopes among the people." — Nelson Mandela

When you question a man's integrity, you can expect a fight." — Nelson Mandela

Education was the enemy of prejudice." — Nelson Mandela

Everything is always impossible until someone does it." — Nelson Mandela

It is what we make out of what we have, not what we are given, that separates one person from another." — Nelson Mandela

<h1 style="text-align:center"><u>Oprah Winfrey</u></h1>

Failure is simply God's way of telling you that 'excuse me, you are moving in the wrong direction.'" — Oprah Winfrey

Your legacy is every life that you have touched." — Oprah Winfrey

Leadership is about empathy. It is about having the ability to relate to and connect with people for the purpose of inspiring and empowering their lives." - Oprah Winfrey

Service and significance equal to success." — Oprah Winfrey

What you focus on expands, and when you focus on the goodness in your life, you create more of it." — Oprah Winfrey

For me, everything that has happened in your life is to prepare you for what is to come." — Oprah Winfrey

No matter the walks of life you ventures, we are looking for the same thing — and that thing is the highest, truest expression of yourself." — Oprah Winfrey

People don't always like you and they are not always happy for you and if you surround yourself with people who are not accustomed to your success, they become fearful; they become scared because you are reflecting to them something that they don't recognized." — Oprah Winfrey

Find your lane. Make space for the flow to show itself. Follow the natural rhythm of your life, and you will discover a force far greater than your own." — Oprah Winfrey

Coaching helps you stop the crazy mind chatter in your head that tells you all the time that you're not good enough." — Oprah Winfrey

The more you praise and celebrate your life, the more there is in life to celebrate." — Oprah Winfrey

People who want the best for you want you to be your best." — Oprah Winfrey

Paulo Coelho

If we only watch the tape of our defeats, we become paralyzed. If we only watch the tape of our successes, we wind up thinking we are wiser than we really are. We need both of those tapes." — Paulo Coelho

A man in search of spirituality knows little, because he reads of it and tries to fill his intellect with what he judges wise." — Paulo Coelho

Winners focus on winning. Losers focus on winners." — Paulo Coelho

Because a life without love isn't worth living. What is a life without love? It's a tree that bears no fruit. It's sleeping without dreaming. At times, it's even an inability to sleep. It's living one day after another waiting for the sun to shine into a room that is completely shut up, painted black, where you know where the key is but have no desire to open the door and go out." — Paulo Coelho

Books bring us opinions and studies, analyses and comparisons, while the sacred flame of madness brings us to the truth." — Paulo Coelho

Nature follows a cycle that's repeated in the human soul: a plant gives birth to the flower so that the bees might come and create the fruit. The fruit produces seeds, which transform once again into plants, which again bloom with flowers, which attract the bees, which fertilize the plant and cause it to produce yet more fruit, and so on and so forth until the end of eternity." — Paulo Coelho

Sometimes you have to lose yourself to discover who you are."
— Paulo Coelho

Negative desires can cause no evil if you do not allow yourself
to be seduced by them." — Paulo Coelho

Energy is to be found in the tiniest things man encounters in
his path..." — Paulo Coelho

God lives in those places where they allow Him to enter." —
Paulo Coelho

Prayers are the branches of a tree, whose roots are called faith.
There can be faith without prayer. But there can be no prayer
without faith." — Paulo Coelho

Only courage in walking the path makes the path reveal
itself." — Paulo Coelho

There are people who insist that they be right about even
minor details. They often do not permit themselves to make a
mistake. What they accomplish with that attitude is a fear of
moving ahead. Fear of making a mistake is the door that locks
us into the castle of mediocrity. If we are able to overcome that
fear, we have taken an important step in the direction of our
freedom." — Paulo Coelho

Fight because you need to fight, because you're facing a battle.
Fight because you are at peace with the universe, with the
planets, the suns that explode and the stars that shrink and
flare out forever. Fight to fulfill your destiny, without giving
thought to gain or profit, losses or stratagems, victories or
defeats." — Paulo Coelho

All roads lead to the same place. But choose your own, and follow it to the end. Do not try to walk every road." — Paulo Coelho

When a tree is laden with fruit, its branches bend to touch the ground. The truly wise is he who is humble. When a tree bears no fruit, its branches are arrogant and haughty. The foolish man always believes that he is better than others." — Paulo Coelho

We are not the judges of the dreams of others. In order to have faith in our own path, it is not necessary to prove that another's path is wrong. One who does that does not believe in his own steps." — Paulo Coelho

The spiritual path is like a fire that burns before us. A man who wants to light the fire has to bear with the disagreeable smoke that makes it difficult for him to breathe, and brings tears to his eyes. That is how his faith is rediscovered. However, once the fire is rekindled, the smoke disappears, and the flames illuminate everything around him —providing heat and tranquility." — Paulo Coelho

If you are traveling the road of your dreams, be committed to it. Do not leave an open door to be used as an excuse such as, 'Well, this isn't exactly what I wanted. 'Therein are contained the seeds of defeat.'" — Paulo Coelho

Walk your path. Even if your steps have to be uncertain, even if you know that you could be doing it better. If you accept your possibilities in the present, there is no doubt that you will improve in the future. But if you deny that you have limitations, you will never be rid of them." — Paulo Coelho

Confront your path with courage, and don't be afraid of the criticism of others. And, above all, don't allow yourself to become paralyzed by self—criticism." — Paulo Coelho

Anyone who would rob for me, would rob from me." — Paulo Coelho

Fear is not a sign of cowardice. It is fear that allows us be brave and dignified in the face of life's situations. Someone who experiences fear —and despite the fear goes on, without allowing it to intimidate him —is giving proof of valiance. But someone who tackles difficult situations without taking the danger into account, is proving only his irresponsibility." — Paulo Coelho

If you are alive, you have to shake your arms, jump around, make noise, laugh and talk to people. Because life is exactly the opposite of death. To die is to remain forever in the same position. If you are too quiet, you are not living." — Paulo Coelho

It is more important to live fully, and allow time to reveal to us the secrets of our existence. If we are too concerned with making sense of life, we prevent nature from acting, and we become unable to read God's signs." — Paulo Coelho

God mixes shadow and light to see if the Earth has the courage to go on turning. If the Earth is not frightened by the darkness, night passes — — a new sun shines the next day." — Paulo Coelho

Each time you take a step forward, you will feel fear at what you'll find." — Paulo Coelho

Life is enthusiasm. Try to remember where it was that you hid away your enthusiasm." — Paulo Coelho

Peter Drucker

The customer is the foundation of business and keeps it in existence." — Peter Drucker

You cannot manage time, you can only manage yourself." — Peter Drucker

The better a man is, the more mistakes he will make, for the more new things he will try." — Peter Drucker

There is nothing so useless as doing efficiently that which should not be done at all." — Peter Drucker

The great mystery isn't that people do things badly but that they occasionally do a few things well. The only thing that is universal is incompetence. Strength is always specific! Nobody ever commented, for example, that the great violinist Jascha Heifetz probably couldn't play the trumpet well." — Peter Drucker

Meetings are a symptom of bad organisations. The fewer the meetings, the better. Meetings are, by definition, a concession to a deficient organisation. For one either meets or one works." — Peter Drucker

Anything more than 25 percent of managerial time spent in meetings is a sign of mal−organization." — Peter Drucker

Persistence is firmly sticking to something for a prolonged period of time, even as you encounter things that try to unstick you. It's the tenacity to adhere to a course of action even in the face of obstacles. It is not enough to just start; you need stick with it until it's done." — Peter Hollins

False hope is about controlling your expectations. When you can have realistic hopes, you can actually achieve, which leads to confidence, competence, and skill. Anything else is just setting yourself up for heartbreak and failure, which tends to not be productive. Don't shoot too high, but don't shoot too low; otherwise, you'll grow bored and unengaged. Just remember that your goals can be entirely different from your expectations." — Peter Collins

Many of the goals worth aiming for in life call for not just a sprint but a marathon. If your heart is not fit enough to run the length of it, then you will find yourself stopping halfway through and giving up before you reach the finish line." — Peter Collins

Overthinking is a silent killer of joy, hope, and reason. It kills your positivity and desire to carry on. Overthinking makes you inevitably fixate on the negative because they are so easy to find, and your entire worldview eventually goes dark." — Peter Collins

A lifetime string of "laters" ends up being woven into the noose of "never." — Peter Collins

Worrying is when you ruminate on problems, real or imagined. This takes you out of the present, which you have control over, and puts you into the future or past, which you have zero control over." — Peter Collins

What is motivation? Things that really matter to you and are near and dear to your heart. Things that make you actually want to work toward your goal. Things that not only drive you, but also discourage you from giving up." — Peter Collins

You might believe that you control the majority of your choices, but in reality, that isn't the case. Instead, a significant amount of your actions are just responses to your environment." — Peter Collins

<u>Plato</u>

True knowledge is a whole, and is at rest; consistency and universality are the tests of truth." — Plato

For a man to conquer himself is the first and noblest of all victories." – Plato

Thinking is the soul talking to itself." — Plato

Love, like drunkenness and madness, is a tyranny; and the tyrannical man, whether made by nature or habit, is just a drinking, lusting, furious sort of animal." — Plato

He who begins by weeping at the sorrows of others, will end by weeping at his own." — Plato

Not pleasure and pain, but law and reason shall rule in our State." — Plato

Justice is to happiness what the implement of the workman is to his work." — Plato

'Goods are arranged into three classes: what are desirable in themselves, what are desirable in themselves and there results and what are desirable in there results alone." — Plato

To do injustice is said to be a good; to suffer injustice is an evil." — Plato

...men try to live in common, but the personal feeling is always breaking in." — Plato

Pure pleasure then is not the absence of pain, nor pure pain the absence of pleasure; although most of the pleasures which reach the mind through the body are reliefs of pain, and have not only their reactions when they depart, but their anticipations before they come." — Plato

For no government of men depends solely upon force; without some corruption of literature and morals – some appeal to the imagination of the masses – some pretence to the favour of heaven – some element of good giving power to evil, tyranny, even for a short time, cannot be maintained." — Plato

The improvement of the human race is the growth and enlightenment of the human mind." — Plato

There cannot be health of body without health of mind; nor health of mind without the sense of duty and the love of truth (Charm)." — Plato

Few persons would deny that we bring into the world an inheritance of mental and physical qualities derived first from our parents, or through them from some remoter ancestor, secondly from our race, thirdly from the general condition of mankind into which we are born." — Plato

For what we have received from our ancestors is only a fraction of what we are, or may become." — Plato

Population is the most untameable force in the political and social world." — Plato

The beginning of a great religion, whether Christian or Gentile, has not been 'wood or stone,' but a spirit moving in the hearts of men." — Plato

For nature too is a form of art; and a breath of the fresh air or a single glance at the varying landscape would in an instant revive and re-illumine the extinguished spark of poetry in the human breast." — Plato

Feeling too and thought are not really opposed; for he who thinks must feel before he can execute. And the highest thoughts, when they become familiarized to us, are always tending to pass into the form of feeling " - Plato

Those who feast only on earthly food, are always going at random up to the middle and down again; but they never pass into the true upper world, or have a taste of true pleasure." — Plato

The first principle which runs through all art and nature is simplicity; this also is to be the rule of human life." — Plato

A just society can only be upheld when the individuals are morally educated." — Plato

...for he who is of a calm and happy nature will hardly feel the pressure of age, but to him who is of an opposite disposition youth and age are equally a burden." — Plato

A house that is divided against itself cannot stand; two men who quarrel detract from one another's strength, and he who is at war with himself is the enemy of himself and the gods." — Plato

...evil is not a principle of strength, but of discord and dissolution." — Plato.

Hope cherishes the soul of him who lives in justice and holiness, and is the nurse of his age and the companion of his journey;- hope which is mightiest to sway the restless soul of man.' — Plato

...there are two classes of persons: one class of those who will agree with you and will take your words as a revelation; another class to whom they will be utterly unmeaning, and who will naturally deem them to be idle tales, for they see no sort of profit which is to be obtained from them." — Plato

For an oracle says that when a man of brass or iron guards the State, it will be destroyed." — Plato

The eye cannot be cured without the rest of the body, nor the body without the mind (Charm)." — Plato

...the wise man speaks with authority when he approves of his own life." — Plato

...how would a man profit if he received gold and silver on the condition that he was to enslave the noblest part of him to the worst?" — Plato

...for that the good poet cannot compose well unless he knows his subject, and that he who has not this knowledge can never be a poet." — Plato

Imitation imitates the actions of men, whether voluntary or involuntary, on which, as they imagine, a good or bad result has ensued, and they rejoice or sorrow accordingly." — Plato

Your genius will not be allotted to you, but you will choose your genius; and let him who draws the first lot have the first choice, and the life which he chooses shall be his destiny." — Plato

Your mind has a soil deep and fertile, out of which spring his prudent counsels.' — Plato

An empty vessel makes the loudest sound, so they that have the least wit are the greatest babblers." – Plato

<u>**Ralph Waldo Emerson**</u>

In fact, the only sin which we never forgive in each other is difference of opinion." — Ralph Waldo Emerson

Trust men and they will be true to you, even though they make an exemption in your favor in all their rules of trade." — Ralph Waldo Emerson

Society everywhere is in conspiracy against the manhood of everyone. Who so would be man must be a non-conformist." — Ralph Waldo Emerson

You cannot do a kindness too soon, for you never know how soon it will be too late." — Ralph Waldo Emerson

I have never met a man who was not my superior in some particular." — Ralph Waldo Emerson

To laugh often and love much; to win the respect of intelligent persons and the affection of children; to earn the approbation of honest critics; to appreciate beauty; to give of one's self, to leave the world a bit better, whether by a healthy child, a garden patch or a redeemed social condition; to have played and laughed with enthusiasm and sung with exultation; to know even one life has breathed easier because you have lived — that is to have succeeded." — Ralph Waldo Emerson

It is a lesson which all history teaches wise men, to put trust in ideas, not circumstances." — Ralph Waldo Emerson

When we say no to a temptation, the power of that dead temptation passes into us. It strengthens our will. When we resist a small temptation, we take on a small power. When we resist a huge temptation, we take on huge power." — Ralph Waldo Emerson

Do not go where the path may lead, instead go where there's is no path and leave a thread." — Ralph Waldo Emerson

Shallow men believe in luck or in circumstance. Strong men believe in cause and effect." — Ralph Waldo Emerson

In fact, the only sin which we never forgive in each other is difference of opinion." - Ralph Waldo Emerson

The days come and go like muffled and veiled figures sent from a distant friendly party but say nothing. And if we do not use the gifts they bring, they carry them silently away." — Ralph Waldo Emerson

Fear defeats more people than any other one thing in the world." — Ralph Waldo Emerson

<u>**Rick Warren**</u>

One reason most books don't transform us is that we are so eager to read the next chapter, we don't pause and take the time to seriously consider what we have just read. We rush to the next truth without reflecting on what we have learned." — Rick Warren

Maturity is produced through relationships and community." — Rick Warren

The purpose of your life is far greater than your own personal fulfillment, your peace of mind, or even your happiness. It's far greater than your family, your career, or even your wildest dreams and ambitions. If you want to know why you were placed on this planet, you must begin with God. You were born by His purpose and for His purpose." — Rick Warren

Many people try to use God for their own self — actualization, but that is a reversal of nature and is doomed to failure. You were made for God, not vice versa, and life is about letting God use you for His purposes, not you using Him for your own purpose." — Rick Warren

...being successful and fulfilling your life's purpose are not at all the same issue! You could reach all your personal goals, becoming a raving success by the world's standard, and still miss the purposes for which God created you." — Rick Warren

You were made by God and for God — and until you understand that, life will never make sense." — Rick Warren

Fortunately, there is an alternative to speculation about the meaning and purpose of life. It's revelation. We can turn to what God has revealed about life in his Word. The easiest way to discover the purpose of an invention is to ask the creator of it. The same is true for discovering your life's purpose: Ask God." — Rick Warren

Your birth was no mistake or mishap, and your life is no fluke of nature. Your parents may not have planned you, but God did. He was not at all surprised by your birth. In fact, he expected it." — Rick Warren

God prescribed every single detail of your body. He deliberately chose your race, the color of your skin, your hair, and every other feature. He custom—made your body just the way he wanted it. He also determined the natural talents you would possess and the uniqueness of your personality." — Rick Warren

God also planned where you'd be born and where you'd live for his purpose. Your race and nationality are no accident. God left no detail to chance. He planned it all for his purpose." — Rick Warren

Guilt—driven people are manipulated by memories. They allow their past to control their future. They often unconsciously punish themselves by sabotaging their own success." — Rick Warren

We are products of our past, but we don't have to be prisoners of it." — Rick Warren

Those who have hurt you in the past cannot continue to hurt you now unless you hold on to the pain through resentment. Your past is past! Nothing will change it. You are only hurting yourself with your bitterness." — Rick Warren

Possessions only provide temporary happiness. Because things do not change, we eventually become bored with them and then want newer, bigger, better versions." — Rick — Warren

Self—worth and net worth are not the same. Your value is not determined by your valuables, and God says the most valuable things in life are not things!" — Rick Warren

The most common myth about money is that having more will make me more secure. It won't. Wealth can be lost instantly through a variety of uncontrollable factors. Real security can only be found in that which can never be taken from you..." — Rick Warren

I don't know all the keys to success, but one key to failure is to try to please everyone." — Rick Warren

Without a purpose, life is motion without meaning, activity without direction, and events without reason. Without a purpose, life is trivial, petty, and pointless." — Rick Warren

When life has meaning, you can bear almost anything; without it, nothing is bearable." — Rick Warren

The greatest tragedy is not death, but life without purpose." — Rick Warren

Purpose defines what you do and what you don't do. Your purpose becomes the standard you use to evaluate which activities are essential and which aren't." — Rick Warren

Without a clear purpose you have no foundation on which you base decisions, allocate your time, and use your resources. You will tend to make choices based on circumstances, pressures, and your mood at that moment. People who don't know their purpose try to do too much—and that causes stress, fatigue, and conflict." — Rick Warren

Purpose—driven living leads to a simpler lifestyle and a saner schedule." — Rick Warren

If you want your life to have impact, focus it! Stop dabbling. Stop trying to do it all. Do less. Prune away even good activities and do only that which matters most." — Rick Warren

Never confuse activity with productivity. You can be busy without a purpose, but what's the point?" — Rick Warren

Purpose always produces passion. Nothing energizes like a clear purpose. On the other hand, passion dissipates when you lack a purpose." — Rick Warren

It is usually a meaningless work, not over work that wears us down, saps our strength, and robs our joy." — Rick Warren

Many people spend their lives trying to create a lasting legacy on earth. They want to be remembered when they're gone. Yet, what ultimately matters most will not be what others say about your life but what God says. What people fail to realize is that all achievements are eventually surpassed, records are broken, reputations fade, and tributes are forgotten." — Rick Warren

This life is not all there is. Life on earth is just the dress rehearsal before the real production. You will spend far more time on the other side of death—in eternity—than you will here." — Rick Warren

One day your heart will stop beating. That will be the end of your body and your time on earth, but it will not be the end of you. Your earthly body is just a temporary residence for your spirit." — Rick Warren

While life on earth offers many choices, eternity offers only two: heaven or hell. Your relationship to God on earth will determine your relationship to him in eternity." — Rick Warren

When you live in light of eternity, your values change. You use your time and money more wisely. You place a higher premium on relationships and character instead of fame or wealth or achievements or even fun." — Rick Warren

...death is not the end of you! Death is not your termination, but your transition into eternity, so there are eternal consequences to everything you do on earth." — Rick Warren

The most damaging aspect of contemporary living is short—term thinking. To make the most of your life, you must keep the vision of eternity continually in your mind and the value of it in your heart." — Rick Warren

You may feel it's morbid to think about death, but actually it's unhealthy to live in denial of death and not consider what is inevitable. Only a fool would go through life unprepared for what we all know will eventually happen. You need to think more about eternity, not less." — Rick Warren

Measured against eternity, our time on earth is just a blink of an eye, but the consequences of it will last forever. The deeds of this life are the destiny of the next." — Rick Warren

The way you see your life shapes your life." — Rick Warren

Your unspoken life metaphor influences your life more than you realize. It determines your expectations, your values, your relationships, your goals, and your priorities." — Rick Warren

Character is both developed and revealed by tests, and all of life is a test. You are always being tested." — Rick Warren

When you understand that life is a test, you realize that nothing is insignificant in your life. Even the smallest incident has significance for your character development. Every day is an important day, and every second is a growth opportunity to deepen your character, to demonstrate love..." — Rick Warren

The greatest enemy of tomorrow's success is today's success." — Rick Warren

Like a proud parent, God especially enjoys watching you use the talents and abilities he has given you. God intentionally gifted us differently for his enjoyment. He has made some to be athletic and some to be analytical. You may be gifted at mechanics or mathematics or music or a thousand other skills. All these abilities can bring a smile to God's face." — Rick Warren

There are no unspiritual abilities, just misused ones." — Rick Warren

There are three barriers that block our total surrender to God: fear, pride, and confusion." — Rick Warren

When faced with our own limitations, we react with irritation, anger, and resentment. We want to be taller (or shorter), smarter, stronger, more talented, more beautiful, and wealthier. We want to have it all and do it all, and we become upset when it doesn't happen." — Rick Warren

Victory comes through surrender. Surrender doesn't weaken you; it strengthens you. Surrendered to God, you don't have to fear or surrender to anything else." — Rick Warren

Great opportunities may come once in a lifetime, but small opportunities surround us every day." — Rick Warren

Where you worship is not as important as why you worship and how much of yourself you offer to God when you worship." — Rick Warren

We can worship God imperfectly, but we cannot worship him insincerely." — Rick Warren

One thing worship costs us is our self—centeredness. You cannot exalt God and yourself at the same time. You don't worship to be seen by others or to please yourself. You deliberately shift the focus off yourself." — Rick Warren

Our families on earth are wonderful gifts from God, but they are temporary and fragile, often broken by divorce, distance, growing old, and inevitably, death. On the other hand, our spiritual family—our relationship to other believers—will continue throughout eternity. It is a much stronger union, a more permanent bond, than blood relationships." — Rick Warren

Healthy families have family pride; members are not ashamed to be recognized as a part of the family." — Rick Warren

Learning to love unselfishly is not an easy task. It runs counter to our self—centered nature. That's why we're given a lifetime to learn it." — Rick Warren

When life on earth is ending, people don't surround themselves with objects. What we want around us is people—people we love and have relationships with." — Rick Warren

The importance of things can be measured by how much time we are willing to invest in them. The more time you give to something, the more you reveal its importance and value to you." — Rick Warren

If you want to know a person's priorities, just look at how they use their time." — Rick Warren

Sometimes procrastination is a legitimate response to a trivial task." — Rick Warren

The best use of life is love. The best expression of love is time. The best time to love is now." — Rick Warren

We are created for community, fashioned for fellowship, and formed for a family, and none of us can fulfill God's purposes by ourselves." — Rick Warren

You discover your role in life through your relationships with others." — Rick Warren

Satan loves detached believers, unplugged from the life of the Body, isolated from God's family, and unaccountable to spiritual leaders, because he knows they are defenseless and powerless against his tactics." — Rick Warren

We only grow by taking risks, and the most difficult risk of all is to be honest with ourselves and with others." — Rick Warren

Whenever you are hurt by someone, you have a choice to make: Will I use my energy and emotions for retaliation or for resolution? You can't do both." — Rick Warren

Frankness is not a license to say anything you want, wherever and whenever you want. It is not rudeness." — Rick Warren

Thoughtless words leave lasting wounds." — Rick Warren

Self−importance, smugness, and stubborn pride destroy fellowship faster than anything else. Pride builds walls between people; humility builds bridges. Humility is the oil that smoothes and soothes relationships." — Rick Warren

One key to courtesy is to understand where people are coming from. Discover their history. When you know what they've been through, you will be more understanding. Instead of thinking about how far they still have to go, think about how far they have come in spite of their hurts." — Rick Warren

We will share our true feelings (authenticity), encourage each other (mutuality), support each other (sympathy), forgive each other (mercy), speak the truth in love (honesty), admit our weaknesses (humility), respect our differences (courtesy), not gossip (confidentiality), and make group a priority (frequency)." — Rick Warren

Peacemakers are rare because peacemaking is hard work." — Rick Warren

Delay only deepens resentment and makes matters worse. In conflict, time heals nothing; it causes hurts to fester." — Rick Warren

Patience comes from wisdom, and wisdom comes from hearing the perspective of others." — Rick Warren

People don't care what we know until they know we care." — Rick Warren

In resolving conflict, how you say it is as important as what you say. If you say it offensively, it will be received defensively." — Rick Warren

Gossip is passing on information when you are neither part of the problem nor part of the solution." — Rick Warren

The good news is that God wants you to pass the tests of life, so he never allows the tests you face to be greater than the grace he gives you to handle them." — Rick Warren

Most people fail to realize that money is both a test and a trust from God. God uses finances to teach us to trust him, and for many people, money is the greatest test of all. God watches how we use money to test how trustworthy we are." — Rick Warren

It is a fatal mistake to assume that God's goal for your life is material prosperity or popular success, as the world defines it. The abundant life has nothing to do with material abundance, and faithfulness to God does not guarantee success in a career or even in ministry. Never focus on temporary crowns." — Rick Warren

Worship is far more than praising, singing, and praying to God. Worship is a lifestyle of enjoying God, loving Him, and giving ourselves to be used for His purposes. When you use your life for God's glory, everything you do can become an act of worship." — Rick Warren

Everybody eventually surrenders to something or someone. If not to God, you will surrender to the opinions or expectations of others, to money, to resentment, to fear, or to your own pride, lusts, or ego." — Rick Warren

Prayer lets you speak to God; meditation lets God speak to you. Both are essential to becoming a friend of God." — Rick Warren

Every time you forget that character is one of God's purposes for your life, you will become frustrated by your circumstances. You'll wonder, "Why is this happening to me? Why am I having such a difficult time?" One answer is that life is supposed to be difficult! It's what enables us to grow. Remember, earth is not heaven!" — Rick Warren

God waits for you to act first. Don't wait to feel powerful or confident. Move ahead in your weakness, doing the right thing in spite of your fears and feelings. This is how you cooperate...it is how your character develops." — Rick Warren

Your character is essentially the sum of your habits; it is how you habitually act." — Rick Warren

To change your life, you must change the way you think. Behind everything you do is a thought." — Rick Warren

Life is a series of problems. Every time you solve one, another is waiting to take its place. Not all of them are big, but all are significant in God's growth process for you." — Rick Warren

You'll never know that God is all you need until God is all you've got." — Rick Warren

Because God is sovereignly in control, accidents are just incidents in God's good plan for you. Because every day of your life was written on God's calendar before you were born, everything that happens to you has spiritual significance." — Rick Warren

Every problem is a character—building opportunity, and the more difficult it is, the greater the potential for building spiritual muscle and moral fiber." — Rick Warren

Character building is a slow process. Whenever we try to avoid or escape the difficulties in life, we short—circuit the process, delay our growth, and actually end up with a worse kind of pain—the worthless type that accompanies denial and avoidance." — Rick Warren

While we worry about how fast we grow, God is concerned about how strong we grow. God views our lives from and for eternity, so he is never in a hurry." — Rick Warren

God develops the fruit of the Spirit in your life by allowing you to experience circumstances in which you're tempted to express the exact opposite quality!" — Rick Warren

There is no growth without change; there is no change without fear or loss; and there is no loss without pain. Every change involves a loss of some kind: You must let go of old ways in order to experience the new." — Rick Warren

Great souls are grown through struggles and storms and seasons of suffering. Be patient with the process." — Rick Warren

What matters is not the duration of your life, but the donation of it. Not how long you lived, but how you lived." — Rick Warren

God never wastes anything. He would not give you abilities, interests, talents, gifts, personality, and life experiences unless He intended to use them for His glory. By identifying and understanding these factors you can discover God's will for your life." — Rick Warren

People rarely excel at tasks they don't enjoy doing or feel passionate about." — Rick Warren

When you are doing what you love to do, no one has to motivate you or challenge you or check up on you. You do it for the sheer enjoyment. You don't need rewards or applause or payment, because you love serving in this way." — Rick Warren

God designed each of us so there would be no duplication in the world. No one has the exact same mix of factors that make you unique. That means no one else on earth will ever be able to play the role God planned for you." — Rick Warren

When we weave the weak strands of our lives together, a rope of great strength is created." — Rick Warren

Our strengths create competition, but our weaknesses create community." — Rick Warren

One key to courtesy is to understand where people are coming from. Discover their history. When you know what they've been through, you will be more understanding. Instead of thinking about how far they still have to go, think about how far they have come in spite of their hurts." — Rick Warren

...money is not taught in schools. Schools focus on scholastic and professional skills, but not on financial skills." — Robert Kiyosaki

Being broke is temporary. Being poor is eternal." — Robert Kiyosaki

The reason positive thinking alone does not work is because most people went to school and never learned how money works, so they spend their lives working for money." — Robert Kiyosaki

If you learn life's lessons, you will do well. If not, life will just continue to push you around. People do two things. Some just let life push them around. Others get angry and push back..." — Robert Kiyosaki

Stop blaming me and thinking I'm the problem. If you think I'm the problem, then you have to change me. If you realize that you're the problem, then you can change yourself, learn something, and grow wiser." — Robert Kiyosaki

You see, true learning takes energy, passion, and a burning desire. Anger is a big part of that formula, for passion is anger and love combined. When it comes to money, most people want to play it safe and feel secure. So passion does not direct them. Fear does." — Robert Kiyosaki

The word 'emotion' stands for 'energy in motion.' Be truthful about your emotions and use your mind and emotions in your favor, not against yourself." — Robert Kiyosaki

People's lives are forever controlled by two emotions: fear and greed." — Robert Kiyosaki

The main cause of poverty or financial struggle is fear and ignorance, not the economy or the government or the rich. It's self—inflicted fear and ignorance that keep people trapped." — Robert Kiyosaki

In an educated society with a well—run government, prices should actually come down. Of course, that is often only true in theory. Prices go up because of greed and fear caused by ignorance. If schools taught people about money, there would be more money and lower prices. But schools focus only on teaching people to work for money, not how to harness money's power." — Robert Kiyosaki

Rich people acquire assets. The poor and middle class acquire liabilities that they think are assets." — Robert Kiyosaki

Once government got a taste of money, its appetite grew." — Robert Kiyosaki

People with vision master the ability to see through to the heart of issues and investments. They value transparency." — Robert Kiyosaki

Sometimes you win and sometimes you learn. But have fun. Most people never win because they're more afraid of losing." — Robert Kiyosaki

Great opportunities are not seen with your eyes. They are seen with your mind." — Robert Kiyosaki

Workers work hard enough to not be fired, and owners pay just enough so that workers won't quit." — Robert Kiyosaki

Texans don't bury their failures. They get inspired by them. They take their failures and turn them into rallying cries. Failure inspires Texans to become winners. But that formula is not just the formula for Texans. It is the formula for all winners." — Robert Kiyosaki

Leadership is what you need to learn next, if you're not a good leader, you'll get shot in the back, just like they do in business." — Robert Kiyosaki

...finding what people miss is key to any success." — Robert Kiyosaki

There is gold everywhere. Most people are not trained to see it." — Robert Kiyosaki

...your world is only a mirror of you." — Robert Kiyosaki

...you must take action before you can receive the financial rewards." — Robert Kiyosaki

The key to becoming wealthy is the ability to convert earned income into passive income or portfolio income as quickly as possible." — Robert Kiyosaki

...the reason so many people fail to achieve success is because they fail to fail enough times." — Robert Kiyosaki

<u>Robin Sharma</u>

Ideas are worth nothing unless backed by application. The smallest of implementations is always worth more than the grandest of intentions." — Robin Sharma

It is one thing to be successful, it is another thing to sustain success for decades." — Robin Sharma

Everything we go through as we travel through a life is, in truth, a fantastic orchestration designed to introduce us to our truest talents, connect us with our most sovereign selves and deepen our intimacy with the glorious hero that lives inside each of us." — Robin Sharma

No one gets out of life without their own ordeals and tragedies." — Robin Sharma

Your past is a place to be learned from, not a home to be lived in." — Robin Sharma

Leadership is for everyone. Each of us, no matter where we live, what we do, what's happened to us in the past and what we're experiencing right now, must release the shackles of blame, chains of hate, leg irons of apathy and prison bars of ordinary that keep us in slavery to the dark forces of our lowest nature. Every one of us must rise each morning—yes, at 5 AM—and do everything we can possibly do to unfold our genius, develop our talents, deepen our character and escalate our spirits. Each of us must do this, across our world." — Robin Sharma

Every hero story needs to have a villain as well as some juicy tragedy along with the triumphs and ultimate victory for it to be a tale worth watching." — Robin Sharma

Every ending marks a new beginning. All we experience happens for a helpful reason. And when one door closes, another will always open for you." — Robin Sharma

I am part of all that is. The great power of the universe is within me. All I desire, with active faith, positivity, expectancy and purposeful conviction, is on its way to me. And if that which I wish for does not come, it's simply because something even better is on its way. I know this belief to be true. All wizards know it to be true." — Robin Sharma

The early morning has gold in its mouth. Rise First. Die Last." — Robin Sharma

To Create Magic in the World, Own the Magic within Yourself." — Robin Sharma

You can't produce magic in your life until you learn the luminous arts of a real magician." — Robin Sharma

Only people in pain do painful things to others. Those who are suffering create suffering." — Robin Sharma

We all know that within every seeming setback lies a distinguished opportunity for even greater success." — Robin Sharma

On the other side of every tragedy lives a triumph. And beyond adversity exists a bridge into enduring victory, if one has the eyes to see it." — Robin Sharma

You don't receive success and influence only because of what you want. You attract it into your life based on who you are — as a person and as a producer." — Robin Sharma

The time you least feel like doing something is the best time to do it." — Robin Sharma

When you enlarge your willpower muscle in one important area, your self—discipline in every other area rises with you." — Robin Sharma

Dream big. Start small. Begin now." — Robin Sharma

Our gifts don't increase when we stay in our safety circles. Nope. Challenge and stretch your capacities past the normal. Muscles expand only when we take them past our usual limits. And then allow for some time to refuel and recover." — Robin Sharma

Life is very equitable. You'll receive from it what you give to it. Key natural law there. So, give a lot more by becoming a lot better." — Robin Sharma

Your past is a place to be learned from, not a home to be lived in." — Robin Sharma

The less we value ourselves and our powers, the less power we have access to." — Robin Sharma

It's time to stop being a fugitive from your highest self and accept membership into a new order of ability, bravery and understanding of the call on your lives to inspire humanity." — Robin Sharma

The primary purpose of life is growth: to be continuously pushing yourself to materialize more of your potential." — Robin Sharma

The leader who learns the most wins." — Robin Sharma

Carrying past pain is so exhausting. We all get defeated — and sometimes nearly devastated by life." — Robin Sharma

One can have no smaller or greater mastery than mastery of oneself." — Robin Sharma

Living in the past steals so much energy from most people." — Robin Sharma

All great artists dream about a future few believe is possible." — Robin Sharma

When you most feel like quitting is the time you must continue advancing." — Robin Sharma

Awesome takes patience. And genius takes time." — Robin Sharma

In many ways, educating others on all I've shared will be a gift you provide to yourself." — Robin Sharma

Neglect your power long enough and you'll eventually believe you don't have any." — Robin Sharma

We need people who influence not through the strength of a large title and by the threat of a big position but via the power of their characters, the nobility of their expertise, the compassion in their hearts and by their unusual dedication to leaving everyone they meet better than they found them. Leaders run less by the selfish addictions of the ego and more by the selfless dictates of our greater wisdom." — Robin Sharma

Legendary performers practice being spectacular for so long that they no longer remember how to behave in non-spectacular ways." — Robin Sharma

All change is hard at first, messy in the middle and gorgeous at the end." — Robin Sharma

What makes the great ones the great ones is they truly understand that daily discomfort is the price of enduring success. And that pushing ourselves hard builds the kind of brain that generates military—grade discipline. It's such a myth that the super producers had easy lives!" — Robin Sharma

You don't have the brain you want, you have the brain you've earned. Or to put it another way, you don't have the brain you desire, you have the brain you deserve—based on how you've been operating it." — Robin Sharma

Your influence in the world mirrors the glory, nobility, vitality and luminosity you've accessed in yourself." — Robin Sharma

It's definitely true that your deepest beliefs drive your daily behavior." — Robin Sharma

No one will believe in our ability to do great things until we first believe in our greatness and then put in the sincere and rigorous effort to realize it." — Robin Sharma

The world is a mirror. And we get from life not what we want, but that which we are." — Robin Sharma

My advice to you is not to put off doing whatever it takes to express your natural genius. Live in a way that feels true to you and pay attention to the small miracles every day brings." — Robin Sharma

With every challenge comes the gorgeous opportunity to rise into your next level as a leader, performer and human being." — Robin Sharma

Obstacles are nothing more than tests designed to measure how seriously you want the rewards that your ambitions seek." — Robin Sharma

To be great you must act great. Nothing can stop a person who refuses to be stopped." — Robin Sharma

Creative people are the real warriors of our society." — Robin Sharma

Many of the people who fueled the progress of our civilization shared the habit of rising before daybreak." — Robin Sharma

Stress hampers your creativity and intellect in very serious ways. When you are under stress, you are prevented from being your best and tapping your real potential." — Robin Sharma

See, you can be in the world all day long chatting endlessly on your phone about one thousand senseless things or you can change the world by exploiting your talent, refining your skills and being a light of upliftment that raises us all. But you can't do both." — Robin Sharma

Become a champion. Remember, happiness is a method of travelling through this wonderful world and not a destination, a place you arrive at in the future. A time will definitely come when your personal power takes you to a place where you have real freedom and joy. This is a place where all dreams come true. This is the place of self—mastery. This is a place called Mega Living!" — Robin Sharma

The life of the caterpillar must end for the glory of the butterfly to shine. The old 'you' must die before the best 'you' can be born. You're so smart not to wait until you have ideal conditions to step up to a work world and private life of stainless excellence. Great power is unleashed with a simple start. When you begin to close the loop opened by your utmost aspirations by making them real, a secret heroic force within you makes itself known." — Robin Sharma

To find your best self, you must lose your weak self." — Robin Sharma

I don't wish for an easy life because there is no growth of my powers there. Give me a challenging life—one that brings out the finest in me. For this makes an iron will. And an unconquerable character." — Robin Sharma

The closer you get to your genius, the more you'll face the sabotage of your fears." — Robin Sharma

The way you begin your day really does determine the extent of focus, energy, excitement and excellence you bring to it.

Each early morning is a page in the story that becomes your legacy. Each new dawn is a fresh chance to unleash your brilliance, unprison your potency and play in the big leagues of iconic results." — Robin Sharma

World—class begins where your comfort zone ends is a rule the successful, the influential and the happiest always remember." — Robin Sharma

The grade of work you offer to the world reflects the strength of the respect you have for yourself. Those with unfathomable personal esteem wouldn't dare send out anything average. It would diminish them too much." — Robin Sharma

The further a society drifts from the truth, the more it will hate those that speak it." — Robin Sharma

The most noble of pursuits is to ignite the fire for personal mastery and life excellence. — Robin Sharma

The minority of exceptional creative achievers operate under a completely different philosophy." — Robin Sharma

Simply make certain that every single step is in the direction of the mountain top and you will get there." — Robin Sharma

Self—mastery is the DNA of life mastery." — Robin Sharma

One of the most essential truths to recognize is the fact that the only limits on what we can achieve in life are those we create and place on ourselves." — Robin Sharma

Circumstances are the creation of people and not the other way around. Peak performers, as opposed to the weak performers, have trained themselves to shape the events of their lives rather than being shaped by them." — Robin Sharma

Every event happens for a special purpose. Every problem is a special challenge from which we can learn and prosper to new heights of achievement. Every moment is perfect in nature, whether you realize it or not." — Robin Sharma

There are simply no limits for a person who accepts no limits." — Robin Sharma

...the place where your greatest discomfort lies is also the spot where your largest opportunity lives." — Robin Sharma

The business of business is human relations, but the business of life is human connection." — Robin Sharma

Without will—power, you become a victim to the evils of procrastination, laziness and sloth." — Robin Sharma

Our society is paralyzed by its tired citizens who lack the energy to achieve what they need to achieve in order to make their lives memorable." — Robin Sharma

Mastery is a state of performance one reaches where every action in the mastered activity reflects unconscious excellence." — Robin Sharma

Any changes in one's life habits cause discomfort at first. Exercising, meditation or the daily habit of filling your mind with new ideas for personal growth might be hard at first. But every time you push yourself past any obstacles, you make yourself that much stronger. The next time becomes a little easier." — Robin Sharma

When all the wisdom of the wisest thinkers and philosophers throughout history is distilled, the purpose of our existence becomes clarified." — Robin Sharma

The purpose of life is a life of purpose and a life of purpose is created through constant service to those around us." — Robin Sharma

The quality of your mind is the quality of your communication." — Robin Sharma

When a negative thought comes to your mind, immediately replace it with one that is positive. Positive always dominates over the negative and your mind has to be conditioned to think only the best thoughts." — Robin Sharma

One of the golden keys to happiness and great success is the way you interpret events which unfold before you." — Robin Sharma

To breathe properly is to live properly." — Robin Sharma

Master your thoughts and you master your mind; master your mind and you master your life; master your life and you master your destiny." — Robin Sharma

From a purely psychological viewpoint, things are always created twice: once in the mind and then in reality. Focus on the positive. Be so mentally tough that nothing takes you off your planned course to success. Visualize and firmly believe in what you want. It will most certainly come true." — Robin Sharma

Be soft as a flower when it comes to kindness but tough as thunder when it comes to principle. Be courteous and polite at all times but never be pushed around. Ensure that you are always treated with respect." — Robin Sharma

There are no negative experiences only experiences which aid in your development and toughen your character so that you may soar to new heights. There are no failures, only lessons." — Robin Sharma

You walk this Earth for but a short time. Why not become devoted to having only a wonderful experience. Why not dedicate yourself to leaving a powerful legacy to the world?" — Robin Sharma

Important but not immediate activities are those which produce long—term, sustainable benefits and include exercise, strategic planning, the development of relationships and professional education. Never let the things which matter most be placed in the backseat as compared to those that matter least." — Robin Sharma

Your life will be elevated by one thing and one thing alone: Achievement. This does not mean that you must strive to make 10 million dollars or build a house in Bermuda. Achievement and life success can appear in peace of mind and a well—developed spiritual life. The key is simply to achieve. Discipline and will—power will make you a success. Cultivate them and treat them as your golden gifts." — Robin Sharma

A habit is like a wire cable. It starts off with a thin thread and through constant conditioning, it becomes stronger and stronger until a time arrives when it cannot be broken." — Robin Sharma

The difference between optimists and pessimists is that the former look for and find the good in everything. A pessimist always sees and remembers the bad." — Robin Sharma

Winners design strategies to benefit from challenges, regroup if they do not work and maintain a burning commitment to succeed at all cost. Winners will always find a way." — Robin Sharma

Perhaps the best way to determine your life goals is to write your own eulogy. Picture your own funeral and what you would like said about you and your accomplishments." — Robin Sharma

Start off small. Small victories always lead to large ones." — Robin Sharma

All satisfaction in life comes from rising to the challenges you set for yourself and overcoming them with enthusiasm and vigor." — Robin Sharma

Believe in your dreams, reach for the stars and have the destiny that you know is yours!" — Robin Sharma

In our society, a great plague is our lack of energy. So many people are living in a permanent state of autopilot and are perpetually exhausted. By adjusting your diet to include more high water content foods, your energy levels and mental agility will improve profoundly. You will finally be able to have the fun you always wanted to have and, ultimately, live the life you have always wanted to live!" — Robin Sharma

Every day is a celebration. Every sunrise is a jewel to be savoured." — Robin Sharma

Every man and woman in this world was born to succeed, be wealthy and be prosperous. The potential for prosperity is one of your most essential human qualities, whether you realize it or not. If there is not an abundance of all that you desire in your life, do something about it and do something this very day. It begins by tapping the hidden and magical powers of that part of your mind that you may not even know exists: your subconscious mind." — Robin Sharma

The quality of your life is determined by your interpretation of what happens to you." — Robin Sharma

Happiness does not come from relaxing and doing nothing. Happiness only comes from achieving and knowing that every day of your life you are getting better and better.

The real secret of longevity is to grow younger by living with passion, zest and enthusiasm." — Robin Sharma

Happiness is a habit. Happiness is not something which develops because you win the lottery or get a great job. Some of the world's happiest people are its poorest or ones that have endured tremendous hardship. But they developed the habit of looking for the positive in everything." — Robin Sharma

The quality of your life is the quality of your interpretation of problems and challenges. The way you see events determines your happiness and your level of success. Your attitude determines your altitude. Once you have developed a winner's mindset, nothing will stop you." — Robin Sharma

Remember, it is not the snake bite that kills but the venom which circulates afterwards that is fatal. Do not let the snakebite of another person release any venom inside of you. You can control its entry and you are responsible for every thought in your mind." — Robin Sharma

Part of your job now becomes unleashing the greatness in people who have never seen the greatness within themselves." — Robin Sharma

Difficult times are the ones that reveal what you are made of — and what kind of leader you actually are." — Robin Sharma

Everyone has a story that is worth hearing. And knows some lesson worth learning." — Robin Sharma

One of the deepest of all human hungers is the hunger to be understood. We all have a voice inside of us. We all want to express it. And when we feel that someone's taken the time to hear and acknowledge it, we open ourselves up to that person. Our trust, respect, and outright appreciation for that person soars." — Robin Sharma

Blood, sweat, and tears are necessary to reach dreams, hopes and joys." — Robin Sharma

I know that people can ridiculously great in their lives until they first feel ridiculously great within their inner lives." — Robin Sharma

Put people first, and everything takes care of itself in so many ways." — Robin Sharma

It would be sheer madness to think you can get by using the same old tactics in a completely new world. And those who resist changing and fearfully hang on to tradition will become extinct, like other dinosaurs who just couldn't evolve as conditions shifted millions of years ago." — Robin Sharma

New conditions call for difficult technique. You need to adapt." — Robin Sharma

The fear you move through when you go through the edge of your limits actually causes your limits to expand. And that expansion not only translates into far better work but much greater performance in every other area of your life." — Robin Sharma

Victims recite problems. Leaders present solutions." — Robin Sharma

The best people always seem to have the biggest libraries." — Robin Sharma

...in the middle of difficulty lives opportunities." — Robin Sharma

...getting lost along your path is a part of finding the path you are meant to be on. Sometimes we need to get off track before we can develop the clarity to be on track." — Robin Sharma

Age is just a state of mind anyway — a label the tribe uses to pigeonhole people and to place limits on all they can be. I choose not to govern any life according to labels." — Robin Sharma

The highest of all human abilities is the ability each one of us has to choose how we respond to the environment we find ourselves within." — Robin Sharma

Leadership has nothing to do with what you get or where you sit. Leadership is a lot more about how brilliantly you work and how masterfully you behave." — Robin Sharma

...every single one of us alive in the world today has unrecognised powers and disowned potential that are far superior to the power conferred by a title. Once you learn how to awaken and then apply those powers, every element of your life will explode into success." — Robin Sharma

Great people were driven by the challenge. By the chance to push the envelope. By the desire to do something uncommonly great. And that's the drive that made them legends." — Robin Sharma

You can't be creative and innovative and all that juicy stuff if you are too scared to think, feel and be different." — Robin Sharma

Leaders are those individuals who do the things that failures are not willing to do — even though they might not like doing them either." — Robin Sharma

Repetition is a powerful teaching tactic. Through repetition, a new idea can quickly become integrated as a new belief. And since it is so important that you install the core belief that you don't have to have a little to show leadership in all you do, you will be hearing that idea over and over again." — Robin Sharma

Finding the center of strength within ourselves is in the long run the best contribution we can make to our fellow men." — Robin Sharma

True human heartbreak is reaching your final moments and realising that you wasted the most important gift that was given to you — the chance to present your magnificence to the world around." — Robin Sharma

... life's simplest pleasures are life's most difficult ones." — Robin Sharma

Too many among us takes the job we have for granted and fail to appreciate all the positive aspects they contain. We wish for something better rather than realising that often everything we are actually searching for lies exactly where we are." — Robin Sharma

It is impossible to build a tribute to success on the foundation of excuses." — Robin Sharma

Leadership is about having an unshakable faith in your vision and unrelenting confidence in your power to make positive change happen." — Robin Sharma

Great people construct monuments with the stones their critics throw at them, you know." — Robin Sharma

Nothing fails like success, because the higher you rise, the easier it becomes to stop pushing the envelope, challenging the status quo, and keeping your focus." — Robin Sharma

Beliefs are nothing more than thoughts we have repeated over and over until we have made them into personal truths...beliefs inevitably become a self—fulfilling prophecy." — Robin Sharma

Ideas are ultimately worthless unless you activate them with focused and consistent action. The best leader never leave the site of a good idea without doing something — no matter how small — to breathe some life into it. Lots of people have good ideas. But the masters become masters because they had the courage and conviction to act on ideas." — Robin Sharma

Every one of us has at our core a well of courage just begging to be tapped. We all want to be superheroes in some form or another and have the capacity of character to keep going when everyone around us is ready to give up." — Robin Sharma

Those who are clinging to the old ways of doing things and frightened of change will join hands and become your loudest critics. They will claim you are doing something that's wrong, rocking the boat, and basically being abnormal. And that would be true." — Robin Sharma

Take some intelligent risks and have the courage to concentrate your greatest abilities your largest abilities on your largest opportunities, even if thought frightens you." — Robin Sharma

The brave don't run. Never forget that. The brave eat their fear before their fear eat them." — Robin Sharma

We all have our own Everests lurking deep within our hearts. You need to be dedicated to climbing them every day. Remember, you will never know how high you can climb if you don't even try. And you are not truly alive unless you are pushing risk and eating your fear." — Robin Sharma

Running away from difficult scenario never made anyone a hero." — Robin Sharma

...complacency has now become primary enemy of victory." — Robin Sharma

If everything is under control, you are going too slow...it is so important: things really do need to fall apart before they can be rebuilt." — Robin Sharma

This time, like all times, is a good time, if we know what to do with it." — Robin Sharma

Where you focus on grows. And where your words go, your energy flows." — Robin Sharma

It takes a ton of security to speak about your insecurities. And the moment you become aware of your fears by putting words to them is the moment they lose of the power they hold over you." — Robin Sharma

Sometimes success is not about making the right decision — it is more about making some decision — and then moving it forward with speed and elegance." — Robin Sharma

Greatness on the outside begins within. You can't unleash peak performance at work until you feel like performing at your peak. You can't show world—class toughness against competition if you don't have mental toughness within yourself." — Robin Sharma

Do the inner work required to make your character richer, your intentions purer, and your acts bigger. Train hard to get your health into high gear so that each day you are full of energy and radiant I'm vitality. Success belongs to the energetic." — Robin Sharma

Life is a blink. It all rushes by in a fast little flash, when you really get down to it. The time to think about your legacy and how you want to be remembered is not on your last day, but now." — Robin Sharma

In this materialistic world, we chase titles, fast cars, and big bank accounts in a search for greatness when, in truth, all that we really want we already have. The excellence and the happiness we crave is inside of us. We are looking for it all in the wrong places: in position, in social status, and in things like net worth." — Robin Sharma

<u>**Shakhti Gawain**</u>

Living in the light involves traveling into the darker places within ourselves, and shining the light of our consciousness into them so that we can truly love and express all that we are." — Shakhti Gawain

Each of us has experience within us; the words we used to describe it are merely the labels that suit us best." — Shakhti Gawain

When we go against ourselves, we experience only effort and struggle; when we surrender to life, we feel passion, aliveness, and flow." — Shakhti Gawain

Death, when we choose it, will not be a tragedy, but a conscious transition into another realm." — Shakhti Gawain

The people and things around you will reflect you in increasingly positive ways. The more light you allow within you, the brighter the world you live in will be." — Shakhti Gawain

Your intuition is always correct, but it takes time to learn to hear it correctly." — Shakhti Gawain

Pain is a mechanism in our physical body that helps us avoid physical harm or notifies us that a part of us has been injured and needs care." — Shakhti Gawain

Healing does not take place on a personal or planetary level as long as we hide or deny our feelings. All feelings, beliefs, and emotional patterns must be brought to the light of consciousness in order to be transformed. When the light shines into the darkness, the darkness disappears." — Shakhti Gawain

Once we accept the reality of a higher power that is channeled to us through our intuition, it becomes clear that many of our personal problems and the ills of the world are actually caused by not following our intuition." — Shakhti Gawain

If we love all the different feelings we experience, they become so many rainbow colors of life." — Shakhti Gawain

We will discover the nature of our particular genius when we stop trying to conform to our own or other people's models, learn to be ourselves, and allow our natural channel to open." — Shakhti Gawain

...if we are willing to take responsibility for our fears and deal with them, we will clear the way for being able to hear the voice of the universe within us." — Shakhti Gawain

The more willing you are to surrender to the energy within you, the more power can flow through you." — Shakhti Gawain

We attract to us and create around us exactly what our hearts and souls truly desire." — Shakhti Gawain

The ultimate key is aliveness. The more the universe moves through you, the more alive you feel. Conversely, every time you don't follow your inner guidance you feel a loss of energy, loss of power, a sense of spiritual or emotional deadness." — Shakhti Gawain

Change happens not by trying to make yourself change but by becoming conscious of what's not working." — Shakhti Gawain

...we can't have any absolute guarantees about a relationship's form. Real commitment allows for the fact that form is constantly changing, and that we can trust that process of change. It opens the door to the true intimacy that is created when people share deeply and honestly with one another." — Shakhti Gawain

There are mirrors everywhere. Whoever you have a connection with is a mirror for you, and the deeper the connection, the stronger the mirror." — Shakhti Gawain

You no longer work just for the sake of making money. Instead, the delight that comes from expressing yourself becomes the greatest reward." — Shakhti Gawain

But the darkest hour is truly just before the dawn. When we finally give up the struggle to find fulfillment "out there," we have nowhere to go but within." — Shakhti Gawain

The more we learn to operate in the world based on trust in our intuition, the stronger our channel will be and the more money we are likely to have." — Shakhti Gawain

When you learn to back up your feelings with action, you create an internal strength and protection." — Shakhti Gawain

When a woman falls in love with a man, she is seeing her own male reflected in him. In her interactions with him she can

learn to strengthen and trust her masculine side." — Shakhti
Gawain

Simon Sinek

Customers will never love a company until the employees love it first." — Simon Sinek

Leadership is not about being in charge; it is about taking care of those in our charge." — Simon Sinek

The goal is not just to hire people who need a job, but people who believe what you believe. If you hire people who just need a job, they'll work for your money. But if you hire people that believe what you believe, they'll work for you with blood and sweat and tears." — Simon Sinek

Competition is about winning. Rivalry is about advancing." — Simon Sinek

There are leaders and there are those who lead. Leaders hold a position of power or influence. Those who lead inspire us." — Simon Sinek

There are only two ways to influence human behavior: you can manipulate it or you can inspire it." — Simon Sinek

<u>**Socrates**</u>

I know that I know nothing." — Socrates

Man must rise above the earth—to the top of the atmosphere and beyond—for only thus will he fully understand the world in which he lives." — Socrates

True knowledge must be elicited from within, and is to be sought for in ideas, not in particulars of sense." — Socrates

An unexamined life did not worth living." — Socrates

For human nature oscillates between good and evil." — Socrates

Whenever we either elevate politics to ethics or lower ethics to the standard of politics, the good man and good citizen only coincide in the perfect state; and this perfection cannot be attained by legislation acting upon them from without, but, if at all, by education fashioning upon them." — Socrates

The motivation for every human action is self—interest." — Socrates

What most counts is not merely to live, but to live right." — Socrates

The beginning of wisdom is a definition of terms." — Socrates

There is only one thing I know, and that is I know nothing." — Socrates

Wise people speak because they have something to say, while stupid people speak because they have to say something." — Socrates

<u>**Steve Jobs**</u>

If you are gonna make connections which are innovative, you have to not have the same bag of experience as everyone else does." — Steve Jobs

We should feel the love in the heart of each of us, and not illusions built by fame or money. I cannot take fame and money with me. I can only take with me the memories that were strengthened by love. This is the true wealth. Love can travel thousands of miles and so life has no limits." — Steve Jobs

Material things lost can be found. But one thing you can never find when you lose it is life. We will have to face the day when the curtain falls. Please treasure your family love; love for your spouse, love for your friends. Treat everyone well and stay friendly with your neighbors." — Steve Jobs

Simple can be harder than complex: You have to work hard to get your thinking clean to make it simple." — Steve Jobs

Your time is limited, don't waste it living someone else's life." — Steve Jobs

Your time is limited, so don't waste it living someone else's life. Don't be trapped by dogma—which is living with the results of other people's thinking. Don't let the noise of others' opinions drown out your own inner voice. And most important, have the courage to follow your heart and intuition. They somehow already know what you truly want to become." — Steve Jobs

Innovation distinguishes between a leader and a follower." —
Steve Jobs

Death is the best ever invention of life. It changes your life;
put an end to your life and open the ways for new ones." —
Steve Jobs

People think focus means saying yes to the thing you've got to
focus on. But that's not what it means at all. It means saying
no to the hundred other good ideas that there are. You have to
pick carefully. I'm actually as proud of the things we haven't
done as the things I have done. Innovation is saying no to
1,000 things." — Steve Jobs

I didn't see it then, but it turned out that getting fired from
Apple was the best thing that could have ever happened to
me." — Steve Jobs

<u>Thomas Edison</u>

If we did the things we are really capable of doing, we would literally astound ourselves." — Thomas Edison

The doctor of the future will no longer treat the human frame with drugs but rather will cure and prevent diseases with nutrition." — Thomas Edison

If we did all the things we are capable of doing, we would literally astonish ourselves." — Thomas Edison

Being busy does not always mean real work. The object of all work is production or accomplishment." — Thomas Edison

The best thinking has been done in solitude. The worst has been done in turmoil." — Thomas Edison

I failed so many times that the only thing left to do was to succeed I exhausted all the failures." — Thomas Edison

Opportunity is missed by people because it is dressed in overalls and it looks like work." — Thomas Edison

Having a vision for what you want is not enough…Vision without execution is hallucination." — Thomas Edison

Many of life's failures are people who did not realize how close they were to success when they gave up." — Thomas Edison

Thomas Jefferson

On matters of style, swim with the current. On matters of principle, stand like a rock." — Thomas Jefferson

When governments fear the people, there is liberty. When the people fear the government, there is tyranny. The strongest reason for people to retain the right to keep and bear arms is, as a last resort, to protect themselves against tyranny in government." — Thomas Jefferson

Nothing can stop the man with the right character from achieving his goal; nothing on earth can help the man with the wrong character." — Thomas Jefferson

The care of human life and happiness, and not their destruction, is the first and only object of good government." — Thomas Jefferson

Were it left to me to decide whether we should have a government without newspapers or newspapers without a government, I should not hesitate a moment to prefer the later." — Thomas Jefferson

When injustice becomes law, resistance become duty." — Thomas Jefferson

Viktor E. Frankl

Between stimulus and response, there is a space. In that space is our power to choose our response. In our response lies our growth and our freedom." — Viktor E. Frankl

...life holds a potential meaning under any conditions, even the most miserable ones. " — Viktor E. Frankl

Love is the ultimate and the highest goal to which man can aspire...the salvation of man is through love and in love. " — Viktor E. Frankl

Humor was another of the soul's weapons in the fight for self—preservation. " — Viktor E. Frankl

What is to give light must endure burning." — Viktor E. Frankl

The last of the human freedoms—to choose one's attitude in any given set of circumstances, to choose one's own way. " — Viktor E. Frankl

An active life serves the purpose of giving man the opportunity to realize values in creative work, while a passive life of enjoyment affords him the opportunity to obtain fulfilment in experiencing beauty, art, or nature. " — Viktor E. Frankl

Suffering is an ineradicable part of life, even as fate and death. Without suffering and death human life cannot be complete.

The way in which a man accepts his fate and all the suffering it entails, the way in which he takes up his cross, gives him ample opportunity—even under the most difficult circumstances—to add a deeper meaning to his life. " — Viktor E. Frankl

A man who let himself decline because he could not see any future goal found himself occupied with retrospective thoughts. " — Viktor E. Frankl

Naturally, only a few people were capable of reaching great spiritual heights. But a few were given the chance to attain human greatness even though their apparent worldly failure and death, an accomplishment which in ordinary circumstances they would never have achieved. " — Viktor E. Frankl

Emotion, which is suffering, ceases to be suffering as soon as we form a clear and precise picture of it. " — Viktor E. Frankl

Those who know how close the connection is between the state of mind of a man—his courage and hope, or lack of them—and the state of immunity of his body will understand that the sudden loss of hope and courage have a deadly effect. " — Viktor E. Frankl

In some way, suffering ceases to be suffering at the moment it finds a meaning, such as the meaning of a sacrifice. " — Viktor E. Frankl

Life has a meaning up to the last moment, and it retains this meaning literally to the end. " — Viktor E. Frankl

Those things which seem to take a meaning away from human life include not only suffering but dying as well. " — Viktor E. Frankl

I know that without suffering, the growth that I have achieved would have been impossible. " — Viktor E. Frankl

For the world is in a bad state, but everything will become still worse unless each us does his best. " — Viktor E. Frankl

It is we ourselves who must answer the questions that life asks of us, and to these questions we can respond only by being responsible for our existence. " — Viktor E. Frankl

For the world is in a bad state, but everything will (still become) worse unless each of us does his best. " — Viktor E. Frankl

Fear makes come true that which one is afraid of." — Viktor E. Frankl

Life is never made unbearable by circumstances, but only by lack of meaning and purpose." — Viktor E. Frankl

Warren Buffett

The difference between successful people and really successful people is that really successful people say no to almost everything." — Warren Buffett

You've gotta keep control of your time and you can't unless you say no. You can't let people set your agenda in life." — Warren Buffett

The more you learn, the more you earn." — Warren Buffett

Someone is sitting in the shade today because someone planted a tree a long time ago." — Warren Buffett

The difference between successful people and very successful people is that very successful people say 'no' to almost everything." — Warren Buffet

Never test the depth of a river with both feet." — Warren Buffet

If you don't find a way to make money while you sleep, you will work until you die." — Warren Buffet

If you can't communicate and talk to other people and get across your ideas, you're giving up your potential." — Warren Buffet

<u>**Zig Ziglar**</u>

You can get everything in life you want if you would only help other people get what they want." — Zig Ziglar

The only thing that is worse than training employees and losing them is not training them and keeping them." — Zig Ziglar

A lot of people have gone further than they thought they could because someone else thought they could." — Zig Ziglar

If you believe in yourself and have passion, you can succeed." — Zig Ziglar

Success is the maximum utilisation of the ability that we have." — Zig Ziglar

You can get everything in life you want if you help enough other people get what they want." — Zig Ziglar

You cannot become what you need to be by remaining what you are." — Zig Ziglar

Life is an echo. What you send out, comes back. What you sow, you reap. What you give, you get. What you see in others, exists in you." — Zig Ziglar

You cannot become what you need to be by remaining what you are." — Zig Ziglar